DEATH IN THE TRENCHES
Grant at Petersburg

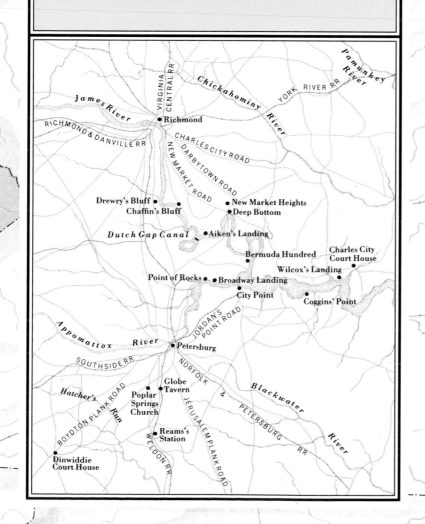

OHIO　　　PENNSYLVANIA

Cumberland

BRINGING LEE'S ARMY TO BAY

In June 1864, two years after General George B. McClellan's failed Peninsular Campaign, the Army of the Potomac, now led by General George G. Meade and the commander in chief, Ulysses S. Grant, had again fought its way to the outskirts of Richmond. Grant had suffered terrible losses trying to flank General Robert E. Lee's Army of Northern Virginia in the Wilderness, at Spotsylvania and at Cold Harbor; now he embarked on a bold maneuver, shifting his line of operations south of the James River and attacking Petersburg (*inset*), the vital railroad center 23 miles below Richmond. Lee had no choice but to follow. The Confederates had ringed Petersburg with fortifications, forcing the Federals to dig in as well. Thus began 10 months of grueling trench warfare.

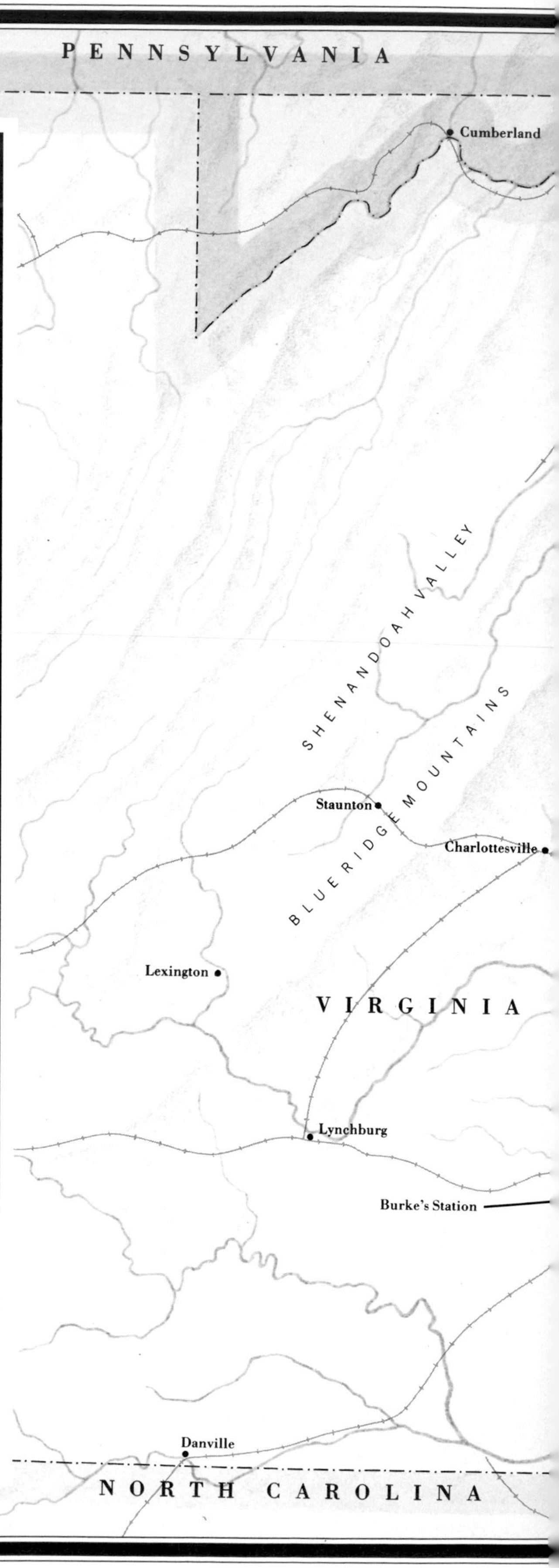

SHENANDOAH VALLEY

BLUE RIDGE MOUNTAINS

Staunton

Charlottesville

Lexington

VIRGINIA

Lynchburg

Burke's Station

Danville

NORTH CAROLINA

Inset map labels

Pamunkey River

Chickahominy River

YORK RIVER RR

VIRGINIA CENTRAL RR

James River

Richmond

RICHMOND & DANVILLE RR

CHARLES CITY ROAD

DARBYTOWN ROAD

NEW MARKET ROAD

Drewry's Bluff

Chaffin's Bluff

New Market Heights

Deep Bottom

Dutch Gap Canal

Aiken's Landing

Bermuda Hundred

Charles City Court House

Wilcox's Landing

Point of Rocks

Broadway Landing

City Point

Coggins' Point

Appomattox River

JORDAN'S POINT ROAD

Petersburg

SOUTHSIDE RR

NORFOLK & PETERSBURG RR

Blackwater River

Hatcher's Run

BOYDTON PLANK ROAD

Globe Tavern

Poplar Springs Church

JERUSALEM PLANK ROAD

WELDON RR

Reams's Station

Dinwiddie Court House

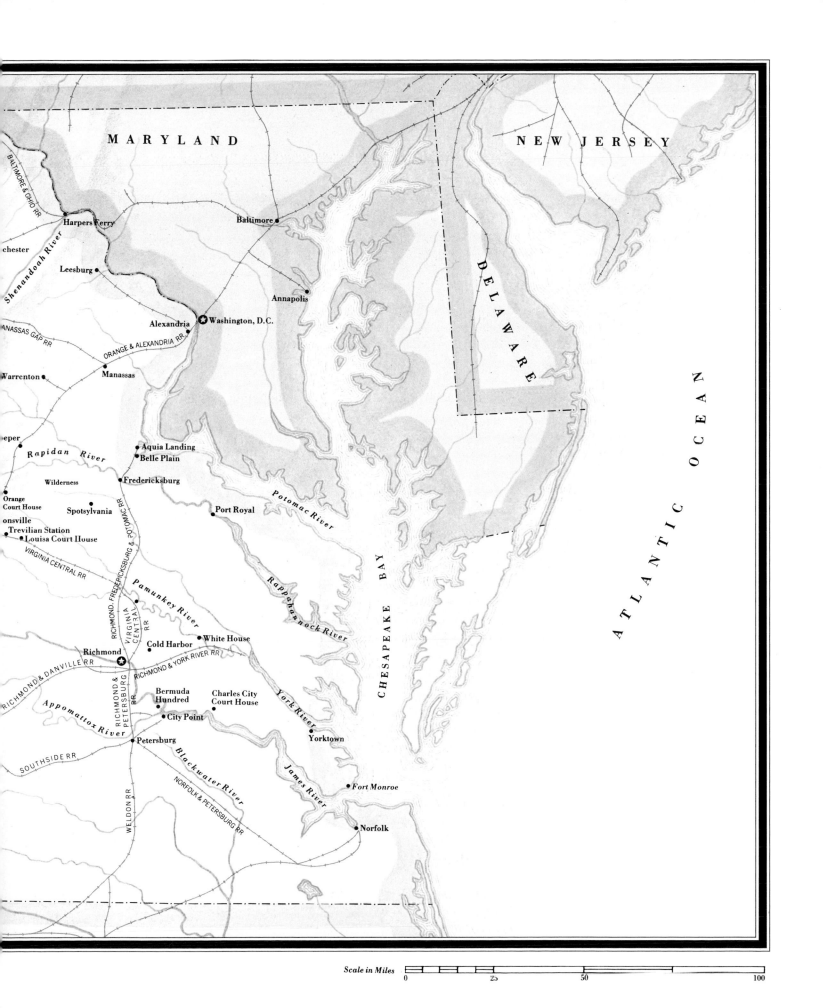

MARYLAND

NEW JERSEY

DELAWARE

BALTIMORE & OHIO RR

Harpers Ferry

Shenandoah River

chester

Baltimore

Leesburg

Annapolis

MANASSAS GAP RR

Alexandria

Washington, D.C.

ORANGE & ALEXANDRIA RR

Warrenton

Manassas

ATLANTIC OCEAN

eper

Rapidan River

Aquia Landing

Belle Plain

Wilderness

Fredericksburg

Orange
Court House

Spotsylvania

Port Royal

Potomac River

onsville

Trevilian Station

Louisa Court House

VIRGINIA CENTRAL RR

CHESAPEAKE BAY

Pamunkey River

Rappahannock River

RICHMOND, FREDERICKSBURG & POTOMAC RR

VIRGINIA CENTRAL RR

White House

Cold Harbor

Richmond

RICHMOND & YORK RIVER RR

York River

RICHMOND & DANVILLE RR

RICHMOND & PETERSBURG RR

Bermuda
Hundred

Charles City
Court House

Appomattox River

City Point

Yorktown

Petersburg

SOUTHSIDE RR

Blackwater River

James River

Fort Monroe

WELDON RR

NORFOLK & PETERSBURG RR

Norfolk

Scale in Miles

0   25   50   100

This volume is one of a series that chronicles in full the
events of the American Civil War, 1861-1865.

The Cover: A Confederate soldier lies dead in a trench at
Fort Mahone. The photograph was taken the day after
Petersburg fell to Union forces, led by General U. S.
Grant. The 10-month siege cost Robert E. Lee's army 28,000
casualties; the Federal attackers lost nearly 43,000 men.

For information on and a full description of any of the
Time-Life Books series listed above, please write:
Reader Information
Time-Life Customer Service
P.O. Box C-32068
Richmond, Virginia 23261-2068
Or call: 1-800-621-7026

THE
CIVIL
WAR

DEATH IN THE TRENCHES

BY

WILLIAM C. DAVIS

AND THE

EDITORS OF TIME-LIFE BOOKS

Grant at Petersburg

TIME-LIFE BOOKS, ALEXANDRIA, VIRGINIA

Time-Life Books Inc.
is a wholly owned subsidiary of

TIME INCORPORATED

FOUNDER: Henry R. Luce 1898-1967

Editor-in-Chief: Henry Anatole Grunwald
President: J. Richard Munro
Chairman of the Board: Ralph P. Davidson
Corporate Editor: Ray Cave
Group Vice President, Books: Reginald K. Brack Jr.
Vice President, Books: George Artandi

TIME-LIFE BOOKS INC.

EDITOR: George Constable
Director of Design: Louis Klein
Editorial General Manager: Neal Goff
Director of Editorial Resources: Phyllis K. Wise
Editorial Board: Russell B. Adams Jr., Dale M. Brown,
Roberta Conlan, Thomas H. Flaherty, Donia Ann
Steele, Rosalind Stubenberg, Kit van Tulleken,
Henry Woodhead
Director of Photography and Research:
John Conrad Weiser

PRESIDENT: Reginald K. Brack Jr.
Executive Vice Presidents: John M. Fahey Jr.,
Christopher T. Linen
Senior Vice President: James L. Mercer
Vice Presidents: Stephen L. Bair, Edward Brash,
Ralph J. Cuomo, Juanita T. James, Hallett Johnson III,
Robert H. Smith, Paul R. Stewart, Leopoldo Toralballa
Director of Production Services: Robert J. Passantino

The Civil War

Series Directors: Henry Woodhead, Thomas H. Flaherty
Designer: Edward Frank
Series Administrators: Philip Brandt George, Jane Edwin

Editorial Staff for *Death in the Trenches*
Associate Editor: Jane N. Coughran (pictures)
Staff Writers: Stephen G. Hyslop, John Newton,
Daniel Stashower, David S. Thomson
Researchers: Harris J. Andrews, Jane A. Martin
(principals); Brian C. Pohanka
Copy Coordinator: Jayne E. Rohrich
Picture Coordinator: Betty H. Weatherley
Editorial Assistant: Donna Fountain
Special Contributors: Elissa E. Baldwin (design),
Thomas A. Lewis (text)

Editorial Operations
Copy Chief: Diane Ullius
Editorial Operations: Caroline A. Boubin (manager)
Production: Celia Beattie
Quality Control: James J. Cox (director)
Library: Louise D. Forstall

Correspondents: Elisabeth Kraemer-Singh (Bonn);
Maria Vincenza Aloisi, Josephine du Brusle (Paris);
Ann Natanson (Rome).

The Author:
William C. Davis was for 13 years editor of the *Civil War
Times Illustrated* and is the author or editor of more than 20
books on the Civil War, among them *Battle at Bull Run,
The Orphan Brigade* and *The Deep Waters of the Proud,* the
first in a three-volume narrative of the War. He is also
editor of the six-volume photographic history of the conflict, *The Image of War: 1861-1865.*

The Consultants:
Colonel John R. Elting, USA (Ret.), a former Associate
Professor at West Point, is the author of *Battles for Scandi-
navia* in the Time-Life Books World War II series and of
*The Battle of Bunker's Hill, The Battles of Saratoga, Mili-
tary History and Atlas of the Napoleonic Wars, American
Army Life* and *The Superstrategists.* Co-author of *A Dic-
tionary of Soldier Talk,* he is also editor of the three vol-
umes of *Military Uniforms in America, 1755-1867,* and associate editor of *The West Point Atlas of American Wars.*

William A. Frassanito, a Civil War historian and lecturer
specializing in photograph analysis, is the author of two
award-winning studies, *Gettysburg: A Journey in Time* and
*Antietam: The Photographic Legacy of America's Bloodiest
Day,* and a companion volume, *Grant and Lee, The Virginia Campaigns.* He has also served as chief consultant to the
photographic history series *The Image of War.*

Les Jensen, Director of the Second Armored Division
Museum, Fort Hood, Texas, specializes in Civil War artifacts and is a conservator of historic flags. He is a contribu-
tor to *The Image of War* series, consultant for numerous
Civil War publications and museums, and a member of
the Company of Military Historians. He was formerly Curator of the U.S. Army Transportation Museum at Fort
Eustis, Virginia, and before that Curator of the Museum
of the Confederacy in Richmond, Virginia.

Michael McAfee specializes in military uniforms and has
been Curator of Uniforms and History at the West Point
Museum since 1970. A fellow of the Company of Military
Historians, he coedited with Colonel Elting *Long Endure:
The Civil War Years,* and he collaborated with Frederick
Todd on *American Military Equipage.* He is the author of
Artillery of the American Revolution, 1775-1783, and has
written numerous articles for *Military Images Magazine.*

James P. Shenton, Professor of History at Columbia University, is a specialist in 19th-century American political
and social history, with particular emphasis on the Civil
War period. He is the author of *Robert John Walker* and
Reconstruction South.

Library of Congress Cataloguing in Publication Data
Davis, William C., 1946-
  Death in the trenches.
  (The Civil War)
  Bibliography: p.
  Includes index.
  1. Petersburg (Va.) — History — Siege, 1864.
2. Grant, Ulysses S. (Ulysses Simpson), 1822-1885.
I. Time-Life Books.   II. Title.   III. Series.
E476.93.D38 1986   973.7'37   86-5930
ISBN 0-8094-4776-2
ISBN 0-8094-4777-0 (lib. bdg.)

CONTENTS

A Graceful City Imperiled by War

As Federal forces descended on Petersburg in June of 1864, the commander of the city's home guard, Brigadier General Henry Wise, issued a defiant oath. Petersburg would be defended to the death, he vowed, "on every street, and around every temple of God and altar of man."

Wise's pledge reflected Petersburg's critical position in the embattled Confederacy. Once a remote settlement laced with muddy streets, it had emerged by midcentury as a vital commercial hub, with rail links to Richmond, Norfolk, Tennessee and the Carolinas. By 1860 it was Virginia's second-largest city, with 18,000 residents; it boasted 20 tobacco plants, six cotton mills, and scores of elegant homes and public buildings.

Flourishing prewar Petersburg is depicted here and on the following pages by three local artists: William Robinson, William Simpson and his son William Jr. Their graceful studies evoke a civic calm that would soon be shattered.

A view looking east from the heart of Petersburg reaches to the spire of Hustings Court House, where Confederate volunteers mustered for war in 1861.

An eagle crowns the Cockade Monument, erected in Blandford Cemetery to honor the men of Petersburg who died in the War of 1812. The memorial drew its name from the rosette American troops then wore on their caps. The Petersburg volunteers served with such dedication that President James Madison dubbed their home the Cockade City.

Listing gravestones lend an air of antiquity to the grounds of Old Blandford Church, completed in 1737 and abandoned as a place of worship in the early 1800s. The church found a new use as a military hospital during the siege of Petersburg, which began in 1864.

This Methodist church on Market Street was spared by the Union guns. A nearby Presbyterian church was hit in midservice, however, and the pastor noted that his flock "dismissed itself without a benediction."

Here at the auction house on Sycamore Street, merchants bid for tobacco, the staple of Petersburg's commercial life; across the way at Mechanics' Hall (*background*), the children of the city's artisans attended classes.

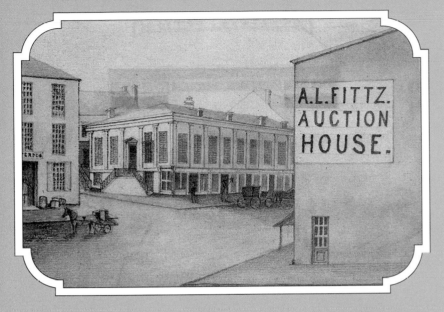

Erected in 1839, St. Paul's Church on Sycamore Street epitomized the popular Greek Revival style of the day. Within its doors in 1850 the body of Senator and states-rights advocate John Calhoun lay in state before being transported to South Carolina for burial.

At the classically proportioned Petersburg Exchange on Bank Street, area farmers displayed their produce to competing wholesalers. The Federal siege throttled such trade and left residents combing the alleyways for edible scraps. "Every particle of animal or vegetable food was consumed," one woman recalled, "and the streets were clean."

A tranquil study of east-side Petersburg includes two of the 13 church steeples that punctuated the city's skyline in the 1850s. A local journalist remarked that if the moral fiber of a place was to be judged by the number of its churches, "then Petersburg must be regarded as one of the most unexceptionable and well ordered communities in the world."

A view from the porch of the John Fitzhugh May house surveys fashionable High Street, largely rebuilt after a fire swept the town in 1815. One resident chaffed that in a single night the fire had "obliterated more eye sores and abated more nuisances than the proprietors of real estate would have done in half a generation."

Touted as the most elegant residence in Southside Virginia, this mansion on Sycamore Street was built for a real-estate magnate, Reuben Ragland, in the 1850s. Ragland was said to have been involved in the slave trade, and the iron railing in front of his home was sardonically called the "manacle fence."

The spacious setting of this home on the corner of Market and Friend Streets befitted its owner, Francis Rives, a scion of one of Virginia's first families, whose members had been prominent in the area since colonial times.

The rocky stretch of the Appomattox River on Petersburg's western fringe was unnavigable, but the swift-flowing waters provided power to major industrial works, including the cotton mill in the background.

Campbell's Bridge, a covered span over the Appomattox, was an important commercial artery in Petersburg. Summoned to work by a bell in the tower of the cotton mill at center, women toiled long hours during the War to turn out sheeting and tent cloth for the Confederates.

The bridge at left linked central Petersburg to the neighborhood of Pocahontas (*background*), which was home to many free blacks. Thriving trade made the city a mecca for skilled former slaves and their descendants: By 1860, more than 3,000 of Petersburg's residents were free blacks.

Bolling's Dam, spanning the Appomattox in the distance below, was only one landmark bearing the name of Petersburg's leading family. Among those to defend the city during the siege was Lieutenant Robert Bolling, who was captured at nearby Dinwiddie Court House in the last month of the War.

An Opportunity Bungled

At the beginning of the second week of June 1864, the Federal Army of the Potomac and the Confederate Army of Northern Virginia lay stunned and quiet, their lines barely a hundred yards apart and a mere 10 miles northeast of Richmond, the Confederate capital. Nothing in three years of war had prepared them for the unrelieved savagery they had just endured.

Throughout the spring the Union troops, lashed onward by their tough new general in chief, Lieutenant General Ulysses S. Grant, had launched one sledge-hammer blow after another: in the Wilderness, at Spotsylvania Court House, at the North Anna River and most recently at Cold Harbor. In 30 days' time they had driven deeply into Confederate territory and had inflicted 32,000 casualties, thus reducing the opposing army's strength by 46 percent.

But the Federals had suffered more than 50,000 casualties — 41 percent of their own strength — and in every battle they had been bludgeoned to a standstill. They had advanced only by marching around General Robert E. Lee's outnumbered but indefatigable host. Now, in the aftermath of the slaughter at Cold Harbor, neither army seemed capable of further motion.

When the spring campaign began, Grant had given Major General George G. Meade, commander of the Army of the Potomac, an order with a memorable, Biblical cadence: "Where Lee goes, there you will go also."

But Confederate General John B. Gordon wrote later that in fact it was Lee who dogged the Federal army.

In the Wilderness, at Spotsylvania and at the North Anna, the Federals had marched away from Lee, hooking around his right flank. Each time they found that the Confederate chieftain had anticipated the movement, had beaten them to their next objective and lay entrenched across their path, ready to stop them again. Gordon wrote sarcastically that what he called "Grant's martial shibboleth" had been reversed and that "Lee was going where Meade went."

Even though Lee was fighting superbly that spring, he was not winning the War. He had lost the initiative, for the first time, to the implacable Grant: Lee was fighting with his back pressed ever closer to the gates of Richmond. Moreover, he was hard put to feed and supply his army and was finding it impossible to replace his casualties, while Grant was able to draw on a seemingly unlimited supply of men and matériel.

Grant was unruffled and confident. "This is likely to prove a very tedious job I have on hand," he wrote his wife, Julia, on June 6, "but I feel very confident of ultimate success." Yet Grant had his share of serious problems. He had not defeated Lee, as he had hoped to do, and the ghastly toll of casualties had worsened the war-weariness that was afflicting the North in this election year.

What is more, Grant had failed to achieve

General Grant studies a map at field headquarters in June 1864. With him are Colonel Theodore Bowers (*standing*) and General John Rawlins of his staff.

A hand-colored lithograph of prewar Richmond by German artist Edward Beyer shows strategic points on the city's outskirts. In the foreground flows the James River, or Kanawha, Canal, used by the Confederates to ship munitions and supplies. The smokestacks on the bank belong to the Tredegar Iron Works, the South's largest producer of cannon.

his first strategic objective of the campaign — to launch all the Federal armies into coordinated motion. He had ordered Major General Franz Sigel to drive south into Virginia's Shenandoah Valley, cut off its abundant food supplies from Lee and then move east toward Richmond. Instead, on May 15 Sigel had been routed by a smaller Confederate force. Grant then had Major General David Hunter relieve Sigel and try again.

In the meantime, Grant had directed Major General Benjamin F. Butler to take his 33,000-man Army of the James up the James River on transports and debark them at Bermuda Hundred — a peninsula formed by a tight bend in the river 15 miles southeast of Richmond. From there Butler was to march 10 miles west, to the Richmond & Petersburg Railroad, and attack either Richmond to the north or Petersburg to the south.

Butler reached Bermuda Hundred on May 5, at which time there were fewer than 2,000 Confederates in Petersburg. But Butler hesitated and worried for 10 days, until a Confederate force of half his strength cut off his exit and immobilized him on the peninsula.

Now Grant himself was stopped again at Cold Harbor, and he was running out of maneuvering room. "Without a greater sacrifice of human life than I am willing to make," he admitted, "all cannot be accomplished that I had designed." Characteristically, Grant regarded this not as a defeat but as an occasion to change his strategy.

Grant now focused his attention on the railroad network that was keeping Lee's army alive. That network had two centers in Virginia, one in Richmond and the other 20 miles to the south, in Petersburg.

Lee's army received most of its food by the Virginia Central Railroad, which ran from Staunton in the Shenandoah Valley to Richmond via Charlottesville and Gordonsville. A branch line ran from Charlottesville southwestward to Lynchburg. In addition, a vital railroad from Danville, southwest of Richmond, and one from Petersburg also met in the Confederate capital. Petersburg was

the hub of three more important lines: the Southside from Lynchburg in the west, the Weldon from North Carolina and the Norfolk & Petersburg from the southeast.

Grant determined to sever these iron arteries carrying the lifeblood of the Army of Northern Virginia. "I have, therefore, resolved upon the following plan," he told the authorities in Washington on June 5. He would send a cavalry force west to cut the Virginia Central for "25 or 30 miles." Then he would make the longest, most difficult sidestep of all: He would move the Federal army to the south side of the James River and seize the rail hub at Petersburg.

It was a plan fraught with peril. Grant proposed to disengage an army of 100,000 men from direct contact with the enemy; march it southward through the swamps on either side of the Chickahominy River; cross the broad, tidal James; and deploy 40 miles away, in the enemy's rear. If Lee were to catch him in the act and attack, the result could be an unmitigated Union disaster.

Grant took pains to make sure that his masterful opponent was blinded to his intentions. The raid on the Virginia Central would help by drawing off to the west Confederate cavalry that might otherwise spot Grant's dangerous maneuver. Butler would lend a hand, as well, by attempting a breakout from Bermuda Hundred on June 9 and, if possible, attacking Petersburg. Three days later Grant would make a feint from Cold Harbor directly toward Richmond. At the same time the real movement — one of the biggest gambles of the War — would begin.

On June 5, Grant sent detailed orders for the first crucial diversion to the commander of his cavalry corps — one of his most trusted officers — Major General Philip H. Sheridan. On June 7, Sheridan was to take two of his three cavalry divisions west toward Charlottesville. He was to destroy the railroad bridge over the Rivanna River just east of that city and tear up the tracks of the Virginia Central from there to Gordonsville, 15 miles to the northeast; then he would work his way back toward Richmond, wrecking the track as he made for Hanover Junction. Every rail, Grant said, "should be so bent and twisted as to make it impossible to repair the road without supplying new rails."

After he had issued these orders, Grant learned that General Hunter had defeated a small Confederate army under Brigadier General William E. Jones in the Shenandoah on June 5 and had occupied Staunton. This was perfect; Hunter could turn east, join Sheridan at Charlottesville, help with the destruction and move with him back to the Army of the Potomac, threatening Lee from the west. In view of this possibility, Grant changed his instructions, telling Sheridan to await Hunter near Charlottesville. Once the

Five miles from the Cold Harbor battlefield, Federal cavalry horses stand tethered outside the Old Church Hotel, which served as Major General Philip Sheridan's headquarters during the first week of June 1864. From here Sheridan embarked on a raid against the vital Virginia Central Railroad that climaxed in the battle at Trevilian Station.

forces met, Sheridan was to detach a brigade to cut the James River Canal.

Sheridan selected the divisions of Brigadier Generals Alfred T. A. Torbert and David M. Gregg to go with him on the raid, leaving Brigadier General James H. Wilson's division behind with Grant. Between them, Torbert and Gregg had about 8,000 troopers mounted for duty. This was about two thirds the number Sheridan had had with him on his Richmond raid the month before, during which his men had bested and killed the legendary Confederate cavalryman, Major General Jeb Stuart.

The Federal troopers drew only three days' rations; they were expected to forage. Each man carried 100 rounds of ammunition with him and slung over his saddle two days' grain for his horse. The small train of 125 ammunition wagons and ambulances carried no additional supplies.

The morning of June 7, the cavalrymen moved north from their camps at New Castle on the Pamunkey River, behind Grant's lines at Cold Harbor. Sheridan intended to follow the North Anna River roughly 50 miles to the northwest, then cross the river and strike the Virginia Central Railroad 10 miles east of Gordonsville at Trevilian Station. From there he would continue westward, destroying the track as he went.

The first two days' march were hampered by oppressive heat and humidity. Scores of horses broke down and had to be shot by the rear guard to keep them from enemy hands. Still, by nightfall on June 8, the raiders had covered more than 30 miles.

The next day, frequent skirmishes with mounted men who, Sheridan wrote later, "proved to be irregulars" added to the Federals' problems. But by the evening of June 10 Sheridan had crossed the North Anna and was camped near a crossroads store barely three miles north of Trevilian.

Now the Confederate scouts became more aggressive, and Sheridan concluded that a large force of Confederate cavalry had succeeded in getting ahead of him. If he was right, there would be a fight in the morning.

He was right. On June 8, General Lee had learned of the fall of Staunton and of Sheridan's departure from Cold Harbor. Lee immediately guessed Sheridan's intent and took steps to thwart him.

The peerless Jeb Stuart had been dead less than a month, and Lee had not yet chosen a permanent replacement to lead his cavalry corps. Two division commanders were in line for the post: Major General Wade Hampton, 46, of South Carolina, and Lee's 29-year-old nephew, Major General Fitzhugh Lee. Lee ordered both of them to go after Sheridan but gave charge of the operation to Hampton, who was senior. The Confederates stuffed barely more than a day's rations into their coats or saddle bags, and at dawn on June 9 they set out to find an enemy force that had a two-day head start.

But while Sheridan had taken a circuitous route to Trevilian, perhaps 65 miles in length, Hampton had only about 45 miles to go. That gained him almost a day, and he proceeded to improve upon the advantage by pressing his command hard. The Confederates rode round the clock, stopping only for two hours to rest the horses at noon, and another two hours at midnight.

It was tough going, through stifling heat. The dust raised by the lead units choked and blinded the men in the rear of the column. "The only water obtainable for man or beast was from small streams crossed," wrote cavalryman Edward Wells, "and this, churned up by thousands of hoofs, was almost undrinkable." But by nightfall on June 10, Hampton and his 4,700 troopers had reached Trevilian Station. Indeed, Brigadier General Thomas Rosser's brigade bivouacked that night on the Gordonsville road beyond Trevilian. Fitzhugh Lee's division, meanwhile, camped near Louisa Court House, on the railroad four miles to the east. They had beaten the enemy to the Virginia Central. Now they had to fight him off.

Hampton was awakened at dawn by Rosser and another brigade commander, Matthew C. Butler. They could hear bugles rousing the enemy in the distance. Their own men and mounts had been at the ready since first light. "General," said Rosser, "what do you propose to do today, if I may inquire?"

Hampton was a master of brevity. "I propose to fight," he answered.

Hampton surmised correctly that Sheridan's course would bring him through the crossroads at Clayton's Store, northeast of Trevilian. From there, two roads led through the heavily wooded countryside to the Virginia Central tracks at Trevilian Station and at Louisa Court House. Hampton advanced from Trevilian with Butler's and Brigadier General Pierce M. B. Young's brigades, sending Rosser's wide to the left to prevent a flanking attack. Meanwhile, Fitzhugh Lee's division was to advance toward Clayton's Store from Louisa. They would meet at the crossroads and together would drive Sheridan back to the North Anna. It was a bold plan, but it could not work.

Sheridan was already astride the crossroads when Hampton started to move. Two of Torbert's brigades, commanded by Briga-

dier Generals Wesley Merritt and Thomas C. Devin, led the Federal advance toward Trevilian Station. Torbert's remaining brigade — Brigadier General George A. Custer's — moved down the Louisa Court House road with one of David Gregg's brigades.

Federal and Confederate troopers met on both roads very early that morning. On the Trevilian road, Butler dismounted his South Carolina brigade and slammed into Merritt's skirmishers, confident in the belief that Fitzhugh Lee would be arriving on his right to help. "We were soon driving the enemy before us in the very thick woods," he wrote later. Moreover, he heard the comforting sound of gunfire to his right.

But Butler was thoroughly outnumbered by the force in front of him. The Confederate advance faltered, then stopped. The dismounted cavalrymen struggled to hold their positions in the thick underbrush, "the enemy meantime pounding us with all his might." No help arrived from Fitzhugh Lee.

The fighting went on at close quarters for several hours. Butler, all the time listening for Fitzhugh Lee's guns on his right, was forced back, step by step. General Hampton arrived with another brigade, but the slow, stubborn retreat continued until the fighting was almost within sight of Trevilian Station.

Now at last new gunfire erupted, but it was not on Hampton's right; it was in his rear. Custer's Federal brigade, all alone, had taken Trevilian Station.

Fitzhugh Lee had barely begun his advance that morning when he ran into the two Federal brigades on the road ahead of him. Instead of attacking this superior force, he changed his route and turned west, on the road that led directly to Trevilian.

Custer was under orders from Sheridan to

General Philip Sheridan (*on the ground at far right*) confers with division and brigade commanders of his Federal cavalry corps. From the left they are Henry Davies, David Gregg, James Wilson, Alfred Torbert, Chief of Staff James Forsyth (*taking notes at rear*) and Wesley Merritt.

try to get behind Hampton. Now, unopposed by Lee, he dashed to his right along a trail that led to the southwest. No one on the battlefield realized it yet, but Custer had got not only behind but also between the two Confederate divisions.

Just as the battle was heating up between Hampton and Torbert, Custer came out of the woods near Trevilian Station. There he found, virtually unprotected, Hampton's ammunition wagons, several hundred horses being held while the Confederates fought dismounted, battery wagons and caissons — all for the taking.

At once Custer sent the 5th Michigan in at the charge. So complete was the surprise that

23

the Federal troopers were carried away by their success. Instead of halting at the station, they pursued the fleeing wagons for some distance and as a result were themselves later cut off, losing many of their number and most of what they had captured.

Meanwhile, one of Young's regiments, the 7th Georgia, deployed between Trevilian and the rest of Custer's force. Custer immediately ordered the 6th Michigan Cavalry to charge, and the men cut through the Confederates to the station.

Then everything changed at once. Hampton, learning of the danger in his rear, pulled Rosser back toward Trevilian from his left. And now Fitzhugh Lee's division entered the fight from Louisa Court House. As Confederate pressure built, Custer attempted to move his men, along with the prisoners and captured wagons, down the Gordonsville road. Captain James W. Thomson's Confederate horse artillery battery, posted on a hill north of the station, found itself in a perfect position to cover the road. As the column of Federals moved in front of the guns, Thomson opened fire, felling horses and riders and smashing the lead wagons. At this moment, Rosser's cavalry struck Custer's right, forcing him back to the station.

Custer was now virtually surrounded. "From the nature of the ground and the character of the attacks that were made upon me," he wrote, "our lines resembled very nearly a circle." The Confederates advanced, Custer's lines contracted and soon "there was actually no place which could be called under cover." With withering gunfire and mounted charges coming in from all directions, Custer dispatched squadrons of cavalry to one crisis point after another. The 24-year-old general rightly became con-

cerned that his command might be overrun. When his color-bearer was hit, Custer picked up the headquarters guidon, tore it from its staff and hid it under his coat.

Sheridan had heard the firing in Hampton's rear, surmised what it meant and knew that Custer was going to need help fast. He threw Colonel John Irvin Gregg's brigade of General David Gregg's division against Hampton's weakened line and forced the Confederates back. Indeed, some of them

In the clash at Trevilian Station on June 11, Brigadier Generals Williams C. Wickham (*left foreground*) and Thomas Rosser (*waving hat, center*) lead their horsemen against a Federal brigade led by George Custer, a friend and classmate of Rosser's at West Point. The long-haired Custer can be seen at right reaching for his headquarters flag, which he saved when the color-bearer fell.

pulled the flag from his coat and proudly waved it over his head. "Not by a damned sight!" he shouted. "There it is!"

The next morning, June 12, Gregg's division began tearing up track from Trevilian east toward Louisa Court House while Torbert's men did likewise to the west, toward Gordonsville. That afternoon Custer's brigade found Hampton's entire force, dismounted and behind log breastworks, across the Gordonsville road two miles west of Trevilian Station. Fitzhugh Lee had marched all night to get around the Federals and had rejoined Hampton at noon. Custer attacked but was repulsed with heavy losses. Torbert fed Merritt's brigade into the fight, then Devin's, but the Confederates could not be budged.

About this time, Sheridan heard some bad news from captured Confederates: Hunter was not coming east from Staunton. Instead, he had headed south toward Lexington and Lynchburg. Sheridan was also told that a Confederate infantry division was in the vicinity of Charlottesville and that a full corps was headed for Lynchburg. Clearly he could not make a junction with Hunter now.

Sheridan had many wounded, most of them from Custer's brigade, as well as 500 prisoners to contend with. His supply of ammunition had been seriously depleted. Weighing all this, he decided to withdraw. Since Hampton was sure to follow, Sheridan would make his way back to Grant "by leisurely marches," thus keeping the enemy troopers occupied for as long as possible.

The withdrawal was slowed by the wounded, the prisoners and the increasing numbers of slaves who were abandoning farms to follow the Federal column. Sheridan's men moved through the oppressive heat, without

were driven into Custer's line as they withdrew. General Gregg moved Brigadier General Henry E. Davies' brigade against Fitzhugh Lee's exposed right flank and drove it back as well. Eventually Lee retreated almost to Louisa, while Hampton and his division drew off to the west, leaving Sheridan in undisputed possession of Trevilian Station.

After the fight, Custer reported to Sheridan. When Sheridan asked him whether the Confederates had captured his colors, Custer

sufficient water and rations, and with Hampton's horsemen following and looking for a chance to pounce. Private James R. Bowen of the 1st Maine Cavalry later wrote of the "intense heat and terrible dust, at times so dense that we were nearly suffocated. It is a positive fact that at times we could not see ten feet ahead, or even distinguish our file leader." It was June 21 when the tired Federal troopers reached their first fresh supplies at White House on the Pamunkey River.

By this time, Grant had already crossed the James. He left behind orders for Sheridan to destroy the supply base at White House and bring its remaining wagons and stores away with him. Sheridan carried out his orders, sending Torbert's division to accompany the wagons and David Gregg's troopers to ride on a parallel road to the west, screening the long train from Confederate attack. On June 24, just as the wagon train neared Charles City Court House, Hampton attacked. Gregg's division received the assault from behind hastily constructed breastworks and held the Confederates for two hours before being forced out of their position. The Federal line fell back, supported by two batteries of Regular horse artillery.

"No enemy could live in front of those well-served guns," recalled Private Henry Pyne of the 1st New Jersey Cavalry. "Slowly backward moved the line, passing the guns, which still covered their retirement." At the last possible moment, the battery commanded by Captain Alanson M. Randol limbered up and dashed to safety. The other battery, under Lieutenant William N. Dennison, remained in place and blazed away. "Take care!" called a passing staff officer. "They will get your guns!"

"Take my battery?" shouted Dennison.

"They cannot take my battery! No rebels on that field can take my battery!" He stood firm as the Federal cavalry withdrew past his position, firing until he had exhausted his ammunition before he joined in the retreat.

The Confederate horsemen pursued, and the battle became a chaos of charges and countercharges through patches of thick woods, the confusion worsened by blinding clouds of dust kicked up by the horses. The fight sputtered to a close — "smothered by the woods," as a Federal recalled.

On June 28, Sheridan rejoined Grant, and the Trevilian raid was over. The gains were hardly auspicious. Sheridan clearly had won the main battle, although losses from the raid totaled almost the same on each side, about 1,000. Yet Sheridan had failed to link up with Hunter. Further, though he tore up

Major General Benjamin F. Butler, his uniform accented by white spats, sits in his tent near Petersburg in the summer of 1864. An astute attorney and politician in civilian life, Butler was too influential to be fired in an election year despite what Chief of Staff Henry Halleck called his "total unfitness to command in the field."

several miles of Virginia Central track, Sheridan's work fell far short of Grant's injunction to "make it impossible to repair the road." The railroad superintendent notified Richmond on June 28 that the line would be open from Staunton to Hanover Junction the next day. Sheridan had interrupted service for little more than two weeks.

Meanwhile, Hunter's efforts to come in on Lee's left from the Shenandoah Valley had produced similarly mixed results. Hunter succeeded in driving the Confederates from the Valley and had moved against Lynchburg, arriving at the outskirts on June 18. Lee took this threat so seriously that he dispatched Major General Jubal Early and his entire II Corps rushing west to meet it. On Early's arrival, Hunter and his army fled across the Valley and kept going deep into the West Virginia mountains, yielding everything they had gained and more. Hunter had failed, but he had drawn off a significant portion of Lee's remaining manpower.

Two days after Sheridan had set out on his Trevilian raid, General Butler had begun to act out his role in Grant's three-part diversion. Butler was anxious to recover from the embarrassment of his previous bungling; as he put it, "the capture of Petersburg lay near my heart."

For a week, Federal spotters watching the Richmond & Petersburg Railroad from observation towers at Bermuda Hundred had been reporting that trains were carrying Confederate troops north, toward Richmond. The defenses of Petersburg had been stripped to reinforce Lee. On June 8 Butler met with Brigadier General Edward W. Hinks to plan a raid on Petersburg. Butler had decided to attack the next morning,

which left the officers who would lead the raid precious little time to prepare. Butler meant to put Hinks in charge of the assault, but while they were conferring, Major General Quincy A. Gillmore, commanding X Corps, entered Butler's headquarters. When he learned what was being planned, Gillmore demanded that as senior officer, he be given command of the raid. As Butler lamented later, "I was fool enough to yield to him."

Hurried arrangements were made on the afternoon of June 8. Three forces were to cross to the south side of the Appomattox—which joined the James just below Bermuda Hundred after flowing past the north edge of Petersburg three miles to the southwest. Gillmore would provide 1,800 infantrymen from his corps, and Hinks would lead 1,300 black troops from his 3rd Division of XVIII Corps. These two forces would attack the defenses east of the city. Simultaneously, Brigadier General August V. Kautz would take 1,300 cavalrymen on a sweep around Petersburg to strike the city from the south.

Believing that Petersburg was defended by only about 1,500 men, Butler thought that each of these thrusts had an excellent chance of being successful. Whichever force broke through first could then move on the flank and rear of the defenders facing the other two. The plan had to be accomplished quickly, however, before the Confederates could shift reinforcements.

The troops moved out that night—and delays began at once. The first challenge was to get the attacking forces across a pontoon bridge over the Appomattox River. This bridge was within Gillmore's lines, yet he and his men lost their way marching to it in the dark. Hinks was there on time, but he had to await Gillmore's arrival; since the plan

Frustration and Failure at Bermuda Hundred

When the Union's General Benjamin Butler launched his raid on Petersburg on June 9, his Army of the James had already been within striking distance of the city for more than a month. In that time Butler and his subordinate officers had accomplished nothing — and they had suffered a thumping defeat at Confederate hands near Drewry's Bluff (*right*).

Ordered by General Grant to advance on Richmond and Petersburg along the south bank of the James River, Butler by May 6 had finished debarking his 33,000-man army at Bermuda Hundred, a peninsula formed by the meandering river. At that moment, fewer than 2,000 Confederates defended nearby Petersburg and the Richmond & Petersburg Railroad, which lay only two tantalizing miles away. Yet Butler devoted his first day to digging trenches and probed only feebly at the gossamer-thin enemy defenses. Over the next three days, Butler sent a few of his 14 brigades inching toward the railroad; but, meeting sporadic resistance, the Federals retreated.

The climax of the timid operation came at Drewry's Bluff on May 16. Butler had decided to attack north toward Richmond. But by then the Confederates, under General P.G.T. Beauregard, had gathered 20,000 reinforcements. They counterpunched hard in a fog-shrouded battle, driving the Federals back behind their trench line on the peninsula and trapping them there. Butler's army had suffered 4,160 casualties, Beauregard's 2,506. Some of the men from both sides who fought at Drewry's Bluff are shown at upper right.

Confederate earthworks at Fort Darling on Drewry's Bluff, overlooking the James River, protect Richmond, only seven miles to the north, from incursions by Federal gunboats. The battle at Drewry's Bluff took place in the wooded country just behind the fort.

LT. ALGERNON E. SMITH
117th New York

SGT. MAJ. E. J. COPP
3rd New Hampshire
Wounded

LT. C. P. PORCHER
27th South Carolina
Wounded

PVT. JAMES W. PRICE
Washington Artillery
Wounded

PVT. GEORGE WILLIAMS
23rd Massachusetts
Killed

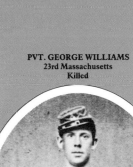

SGT. WILLIAM P. WHITLOW
11th Virginia
Wounded

Though sealed up at Bermuda Hundred, Federal observers could watch the Confederates closely from a 126-foot-tall signal tower. From there, artist Alfred Waud drew a panorama (*top*), which shows the winding Appomattox to the south and beyond it the spires of Petersburg (*right*). Waud labeled other areas that would be fought over in the months to come.

called for the infantry to cross before the cavalry, Kautz, too, was held up for several hours. Thus, though ordered to cross at midnight on June 8, Gillmore did not get his command south of the Appomattox until 3:40 a.m. on June 9.

The operation was not yet under way, but the faultfinding was. Gillmore sent word that he anticipated trouble because the hoofbeats of the cavalry crossing the bridge could be heard "for miles." Forgetting or ignoring the fact that he was in charge, Gillmore complained that no one had muffled the bridge with straw. Butler read the message and smelled doom. "From the hour of getting that dispatch," he recalled, "heartsick, I doubted the result of the expedition."

Gillmore's orders were to wait until daylight, march toward the southwest until he struck the enemy's picket line, drive it in and then attack Petersburg's main works. Hinks was to follow the cavalry south to the Jordan's Point road, then turn and launch his own assault straight west on the city.

"Unless the attack is made promptly and vigorously there will be danger of failure," Gillmore told Hinks at 5 a.m. When Hinks asked if they were to hold any ground gained against strong counterattacks, Gillmore's reply was "No; unless we take them within an hour it will be useless to attempt it and you must use your discretion in the attack." At 6 a.m. Gillmore's men encountered the first of the enemy pickets and opened fire.

Awaiting the Federals inside the city's defenses were barely 1,000 Confederates. They were led by Brigadier General Henry A. Wise, a crusty former Governor of Virginia and brother-in-law to Union General Meade. Lacking any military training or experience, Wise was a purely political general, just like Butler, and fellow Confederates thought about as much of Wise's ability as Federals did of Butler's. Wise was commanding the depleted forces in Petersburg because the Confederates did not expect anything to happen there.

These forces consisted of the 46th Virginia, a few scattered artillery companies, a company of the 23rd South Carolina, a small body of cavalry and Major Fletcher H. Archer's company of local militia. Major Archer later remembered the appearance of his line of old men and boys. "What a line it was!" he wrote. "In number scarcely more than a single company. In dress nothing to distinguish them in appearance from citizens pursuing the ordinary avocations of life." Archer recalled that when he gave the order to load muskets, one elderly man carefully used a pocket knife to open the paper cartridge — the man had no teeth with which to bite it open. When the shooting started, Wise mustered wounded soldiers from the city's hospitals and even released a few score Confederate military prisoners to augment his force. Brigadier General Raleigh Colston, who had been without assignment for some time, happened to be in the city, and Wise gratefully accepted his offer of help.

The Federals unwittingly gave Wise plenty of time to organize his defense. Gillmore had pushed forward slowly for about an hour after encountering the pickets. Then he halted before the Confederate defenses around 7 a.m. Hinks proceeded to the Jordan's Point road, turned and advanced as planned, driving Wise's pickets before him until he came within 600 yards of the main enemy works. There he, too, stopped.

Gillmore was an engineer by training, and an excellent one, who had made his reputation by using artillery to reduce enemy forts. But he had no artillery with him now. Further, he had no experience leading troops in combat. Looking at the formidable earthworks before him, he hesitated. In his report the next day, Gillmore made the assertion that "it was no part of the plan to assault the enemy's works on the right, unless there was a strong probability of success or until General Kautz's attack should divert them."

Hinks, meanwhile, found himself being peppered by a single Confederate battery, hastily brought forward by Wise. Hearing no firing on his right, where he expected Gillmore to be attacking, Hinks sent word that the works in his own front were too strong and too heavily manned. He felt he could not succeed unless Gillmore attacked with him.

Gillmore, who outnumbered the Confederates in his front by better than 4 to 1, replied that he would attack but that both of them should hold their positions and await Kautz's assault from the south.

But Kautz would not arrive for another five hours. After leaving the infantry, Kautz's cavalry had met enemy pickets on every road. This continual, though feeble, resistance slowed the troopers' progress, which had already been hampered by an or-

der from someone — no one knows who — that they ride at a walk. As a result, Kautz did not reach the outer line of Petersburg's defenses until noon. Confident that he could take the lightly defended works, he attacked.

Kautz was facing Major Archer, commanding 150 militiamen posted in two artillery lunettes on either side of the Jerusalem Plank Road. The militiamen turned back Kautz's first probing attack, a mounted charge by the 5th Pennsylvania Cavalry. The Federals dismounted before continuing the attack, providing a lull in the action. Behind the Petersburg militiamen, a clatter of horses' hoofs heralded the arrival of General Colston, accompanied by one 12-pounder howitzer and six gunners from Sturdivant's Virginia Battery. To his dismay, Colston found that the gun's limber chest contained no case or canister rounds — the ammunition of choice against attacking formations. He had to make do with solid shot and shells fused to burst at point-blank range. Despite this disadvantage and the inexperience of his small command, Colston held his position. Soon, however, Kautz had two fieldpieces firing on the Confederates, and he began extending his line on either flank.

Colston was in serious trouble. His nearest support to the left was a mile away; to the

right there was a four-mile gap. Still he held on until troopers of the 5th Pennsylvania Cavalry and the 1st District of Columbia Cavalry were within 50 yards of him. Suddenly skirmishers of the 11th Pennsylvania began to overlap his flanks. Only then, still fighting, did Colston begin to pull back, leaving on the field his howitzer, 50 men killed or wounded, and 35 taken prisoner.

As the remnants of the local militia fell back into Petersburg and took a new position near the city's waterworks, Kautz pursued with two squadrons of the 11th Pennsylvania while the remainder of his command returned to mount their horses. The Federals entered a ravine just on the edge of the city, and when they reached its bottom they came under heavy fire from Captain Edward Graham's Virginia Battery on the heights above. Thanks to Gillmore's timidity, Wise had been able to shift the battery and two regiments of cavalry from Brigadier General James Dearing's brigade, which had just arrived from the Richmond defenses; now their combined fire was so galling that Kautz pulled his advance squadron back and halted his main column.

Although Kautz believed that Petersburg was not strongly held, he feared the defenders could repulse him long enough for rein-

forcements to come in and for the Confederate cavalry to cut off his line of retreat. Hearing nothing from Gillmore's front, Kautz concluded that his infantry supports had withdrawn, leaving him on his own. He saw no alternative but to retreat. He took with him the captured howitzer, but left behind one of his own cannon in the confusion.

Kautz had come within 150 yards of the streets of Petersburg at 1:30 p.m. Just half an hour earlier, Gillmore and Hinks had pulled back to unite their forces. They had missed a golden opportunity. With most of Wise's command shifted to face Kautz's attack, an infantry assault on the eastern fortifications should have been a walkover.

The Federals might not have been able to hold Petersburg for long — Confederate reinforcements were already on their way from the force confronting Butler on Bermuda Hundred — but they could have held the city long enough to destroy public buildings, warehouses, railroad track and rolling stock. Instead, Gillmore and his command retreated to the Appomattox River and began making their excuses.

Butler immediately charged Gillmore with disobedience and military incapacity, re- moved him from command and ordered his arrest. Gillmore requested a court of inquiry; it was never convened, but Grant restored his freedom and transferred him to another command, apparently writing off the affair as a poor performance by all involved.

The attack had been so feeble that it amounted to the least of Robert E. Lee's troubles of the moment. Of crucial importance to the Confederate commander was an awareness of Grant's next move. But Lee's intuitive grasp of his opponent's strategy had deserted him. Then, and for several days thereafter, the Confederate general would have no idea, and no way of finding out, what Grant intended to do.

Grant could not have known how thoroughly he had succeeded in confusing and bedeviling General Lee. Yet he must have sensed something, because he accepted the recent shortcomings of his own operations with remarkable sanguinity. "Everything is progressing favorably but slowly," he wrote to his old friend, Congressman Elihu Washburne. He still had the initiative, and he knew exactly what he was going to do with it. "Unless my next move brings on a battle," Grant wrote, "the balance of the campaign will settle down to a siege."

Crossing the James

"*The feeling here in the army is that we have been absolutely butchered, that our lives have been periled to no purpose, and wasted. I can tell you, Father, it is discouraging to see one's men and officers cut down and butchered time and again, and all for nothing.*"

COLONEL STEPHEN M. WELD, 56TH MASSACHUSETTS, IN A LETTER FROM THE PETERSBURG FRONT, JUNE 21, 1864

2

Sometime before sundown on June 12, 1864, a Confederate picket at Barker's Mill on the Chickahominy River yelled a question toward the nearby Federal lines: "Where is Grant agoing to elbow us again?" He was referring, of course, to Grant's repeated edging around Lee's right flank since the beginning of the spring campaign. What neither the Confederate picket nor his commanding general knew that evening was that the next elbowing was already in progress.

Under cover of the advancing darkness, all 100,000 men of the Union's Army of the Potomac were beginning a ponderous, meticulously orchestrated movement. Five infantry corps, a division of cavalry, 49 batteries of artillery along with their 1,200 caissons and ammunition wagons, and an enormous train of supply wagons were about to vanish from the sight of the Confederate Army of Northern Virginia and reappear in its rear, 40 miles away. It would be the most difficult and daring elbowing of all. The next morning, that inquisitive picket would be astonished to find the lines opposite him deserted.

The logistics of the move were formidable. Federal infantry formations sprawled for 10 miles northwestward from Barker's Mill— on the Chickahominy 12 miles east of Richmond—to Totopotomoy Creek, northeast of the city. The Federal left covered the railroad on which supplies were forwarded from the depot at White House on the Pamunkey River, another 10 miles to the east.

Grant would have to back the entire army out of its lines and away from direct contact with the Confederate pickets without arousing suspicion and march the mass of men and animals southeastward along the Chickahominy to crossing points that were a safe distance from the enemy. Once across the Chickahominy, the Federals would have to march another 12 miles south to the James, which they planned to cross using a combination of ferries and an enormous pontoon bridge that had not yet been built.

The historic James was a daunting barrier to the passage of so large an army. At the chosen crossing place, Wilcox's Landing, the river was 2,100 feet wide and nearly 100 feet deep in the middle; it had a strong current and rose or fell four feet with the tide. Crossing the river would require the rapid construction of a pontoon bridge that would be the longest ever built, not to mention one of the strongest and most flexible.

Contingency preparations for the movement had begun weeks earlier, with the collection at Fort Monroe at the mouth of the James of an enormous quantity of pontoons and planking for bridges, along with a fleet of tugboats, ferryboats and gunboats. Immediately after the fighting at Cold Harbor had ended in stalemate on June 3, firm plans had been drawn in exacting detail.

By the evening of June 12, engineers had scouted the river crossings and had built a new line of entrenchments just behind the

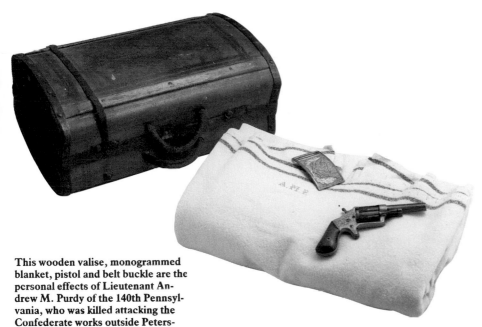

This wooden valise, monogrammed blanket, pistol and belt buckle are the personal effects of Lieutenant Andrew M. Purdy of the 140th Pennsylvania, who was killed attacking the Confederate works outside Petersburg on June 16, 1864. Two days later, Purdy's regiment dislodged the Confederates and helped seize the Norfolk & Petersburg Railroad.

Federal left to cover the movement and to make it look as though they intended to stay. They had also begun dismantling the depot at White House and tearing up the railroad so that neither could be used by the enemy.

Late that afternoon Generals Grant and Meade rode down to the Chickahominy to observe as the grand movement got under way. Already the roads were choked with dust, and the temperature stood near 100°. Even the imperturbable Grant showed the strain. He lit cigars, then forgot that he had done so and let them go out, time and again. He snapped at his staff officers and interrupted them as they made their reports. His aide, Lieutenant Colonel Horace Porter, recalled that Grant was "wrought up to an intensity of thought and action which he seldom displayed." It was no wonder, for once the complicated maneuver had started, his entire army would be subject to a myriad of possible errors and vulnerable to attack. With the sunset, there was no going back.

The first movement was carried out by XVIII Corps, under Major General William F. (Baldy) Smith, borrowed earlier from Benjamin Butler's Army of the James. At sunset Smith's corps pulled out of its place on the right center of the Union line and began the 15-mile march to White House Landing. There the men were to board steamers and ferryboats for the 140-mile passage down the Pamunkey to the York, thence to Hampton Roads and back up the James to Bermuda Hundred, where they would rejoin Butler.

Meanwhile, Brigadier General James Wilson, with one of his two cavalry brigades, led Major General Gouverneur K. Warren's V Corps out of the left of the line and down the Chickahominy. Six miles downstream, engineers were throwing a pontoon bridge across the river at the site of Long Bridge, destroyed earlier by the Confederates. Wilson and Warren were to cross there, then thrust northwest toward Richmond. This was the feint, meant to deceive Lee into thinking that Grant intended merely to elbow around his right flank again.

As the ponderous dance continued, Major General Winfield Scott Hancock's II Corps and Major General Horatio G. Wright's VI Corps dropped back from the main line after dark and took up a position in the new line of fortifications to cover Smith's and Warren's withdrawals. Behind them came IX Corps, under Major General Ambrose Burnside, following Smith toward White House. A few miles short of the landing, Burnside was to turn south toward the site of Jones Bridge, five miles downstream from Long Bridge, and cross the river there.

Incredibly, all went smoothly. The engineers had assembled the pontoons at Long Bridge by 1:30 a.m., whereupon Wilson's cavalry and Warren's V Corps crossed and formed up for the feint toward Richmond. By morning, Smith's men had reached White House, Hancock had set off in Warren's path and Wright, with the rest of Wilson's cavalry as rear guard, was following Burnside toward Jones Bridge. At first light, the Cold Harbor lines were empty.

All day on June 13 the Federals pressed on, despite the heat and dust. Around noon, Hancock's II Corps reached the Chickahominy and began crossing. Even though the men in the ranks still did not know what Grant had in mind for them, their mood was improved just by being on the march again without having to fight for every foot of ground. "By the left flank, once more!" exulted a reporter with one of the corps crossing at Jones Bridge. "Where we go we know not," he wrote that afternoon, but no matter: "All have learned to follow General Grant wherever he leads, and no questions asked."

That evening the whole operation was still progressing without flaw. Around 5:30 Hancock's advance units reached Wilcox's Landing on the James. Wright and Burnside were following, the former crossing the Chickahominy as night fell and the latter bivouacking by the river to cross the next morning. Warren and Wilson were menacing Richmond, skirmishing frequently with mounted Confederate patrols.

The flotilla from Fort Monroe had arrived on time. Ferryboats were ready to begin taking Hancock's men across the James in the morning, and engineers were preparing to throw the massive pontoon bridge on which the rest of the army would cross.

By this time, Grant showed no sign of his earlier tension. He lounged on a blanket beside a campfire, smoking and talking with his staff, calming those around him. When a visiting dignitary ranted over the loss of a wagon, Grant merely commented absently,

not bothering to finish his sentence, "If we have nothing worse than this . . ."

Now it was Robert E. Lee's turn to worry. He had lost Grant completely. That morning, when Confederate skirmishers found the Federal works empty, they had probed for more than a mile and still encountered nothing. Then came the gunfire on the roads leading into Richmond from the east, beyond Lee's right, and it seemed certain that Grant was elbowing again. At once Lee put his army in motion; his columns streamed along the back roads to cross the Chickahominy and cover the approaches to Richmond.

That evening the Confederates pushed back the Federal feint a mile or so, and Lee planned a full-scale assault for the morning. But when his divisions advanced at dawn, there was no enemy to attack. And Lee could not find out where the Federals had gone.

As early as June 9, General P.G.T. Beauregard had predicted that Grant would cross the James and strike Petersburg, but no one had listened. Lee had admitted that Grant might contemplate such a move, but he believed Grant's likelier target was Richmond. Moreover, he confidently asserted that the Federal army could not cross the James without being discovered.

Lee was wrong on both counts. Undetected by the enemy, Federal ferryboats began taking Hancock's corps across on June 14, and his 20,000-man command was finished with the operation by the next morning. Meanwhile, 450 engineers under Captain George H. Mendell began the formidable task of erecting the half-mile-long bridge. Working toward midriver from either shore, the men maneuvered into place 101 heavy wooden pontoon boats. To help steady the enormous floating bridge against the power-

Perched on a sack of oats at his headquarters near Cold Harbor, Major General Ambrose E. Burnside, commander of IX Corps, reads a Washington newspaper in early June 1864. Opposite Burnside with his arms folded is the photographic entrepreneur Mathew Brady, whose cameraman took this picture. A few days later, General Grant shifted Burnside's corps south of the James River to attack Petersburg.

ful current, the engineers lashed it to three schooners anchored in midstream. There they also rigged an ingenious swinging section that would permit the passage of ironclads to protect the crossing point from enemy gunboats known to be upstream. All this was finished in only eight hours, and by midnight of June 14, men, horses, wagons and artillery were trundling across the river.

Burnside's IX Corps was the first to use the bridge, followed by V Corps, its successful feint now abandoned. Wilson and the cavalry crossed on June 16, followed by Wright's VI Corps, which had stayed on the north side of the James to cover the crossing. By the 17th, all of the army except some wagons and their guards were on the south side.

As brilliantly conceived and as flawlessly executed as the movement across the James had been, it was only a part of Grant's current plan. He had deceived Lee for two vital days, but he would have to continue to move swiftly in order to consolidate his advantage. Remarkably, for the boldness and dash required to ensure the payoff that the maneuvers made possible, Grant turned to Butler's Army of the James, whose performance until now had been uninspired.

On June 14, Grant took a steamer up the river to Butler's headquarters and there explained his orders. Baldy Smith's XVIII Corps was to arrive at Bermuda Hundred that afternoon, and Grant wanted Butler to augment that corps to a strength of perhaps

This photograph, taken from atop a canvas-covered supply wagon, shows Federal troops crossing the James on a 2,100-foot-long pontoon bridge installed by Army of the Potomac engineers on June 14, 1864. The schooners at midstream were used to anchor the bridge in the swift current.

16,000 men. Then Smith was to retrace the route taken by Gillmore and Hinks a week earlier and attack Petersburg's works at daylight on June 15. "I believed then, and still believe," Grant would write 20 years later, "that Petersburg could have been easily captured at that time." Indeed, before leaving Butler's headquarters, Grant wired Chief of Staff Henry Halleck in Washington that he would have Petersburg secured before enemy reinforcements could arrive.

Grant ordered Hancock to march toward Petersburg on the morning of June 15. Grant expected to be inside the enemy works by noon, and Assistant Secretary of War Charles A. Dana, traveling with him, wired to Washington that Hancock was on his way. "All goes on like a miracle," Dana added.

By that morning General Beauregard, now in overall command of the scanty forces in Petersburg, was growing alarmed. The one-time Confederate hero of Fort Sumter and First Bull Run had only Henry Wise's force, now numbering about 2,200 men, to defend the city, and only 3,200 facing Butler's considerably greater numbers at Bermuda Hundred. Beauregard learned of the arrival of Smith's corps to reinforce Butler and began to doubt whether he could hold out.

One of the few things in Beauregard's favor was the strength of the fortifications around Petersburg, which had stopped Butler's men once before. An imposing chain of artillery emplacements connected by earthworks and trenches stretched for almost 10 miles, from the Appomattox east of the city, around to the south and back up to the river on the west. This line was studded with redans — triangular projections placed to give the defenders converging fields of fire. Ditches,

abatis and chevaux-de-frise were arrayed before the earthworks to slow any hostile advance. It was called the Dimmock Line, after the engineer who had laid it out, but its strength was largely illusory unless properly manned, and Beauregard and Wise simply did not have the numbers to do that.

The best they could do was to concentrate Wise's tiny command along the eastern four miles of the line, between Redan No. 1, on the Appomattox River, and Redan No. 23, covering the Norfolk & Petersburg Railroad southeast of the city. But to man even this fragment of the line, Beauregard had to space his infantry at intervals of 10 feet. He could not expect to repulse the Federals for long. He could only hope that the formidable appearance of the works, concealment of his weakness from the enemy and a stiff resistance might buy him enough time to convince Lee that the real danger lay south, not north, of the James.

Beauregard soon was given an unexpected gift of time. The Federal assault force under General Smith, consisting of his own corps, Hinks's division of black troops and Kautz's division of cavalry, had left Broadway Landing on the Appomattox at 4 a.m. on June 15, with Kautz in the lead. Once again, the plan called for Kautz to ride south to the Jerusalem Plank Road and make a feint there, while Smith made the main attack from the east. About 7 a.m., Kautz reached the City Point Railroad, a few miles east of Petersburg, and drove in some enemy pickets.

At nine that morning, just as the Union infantry under Smith began driving in Wise's pickets east of Petersburg, Lee was declaring firmly to one of Beauregard's aides that Grant had not crossed the James, nor had Smith reinforced Butler. But the fiery

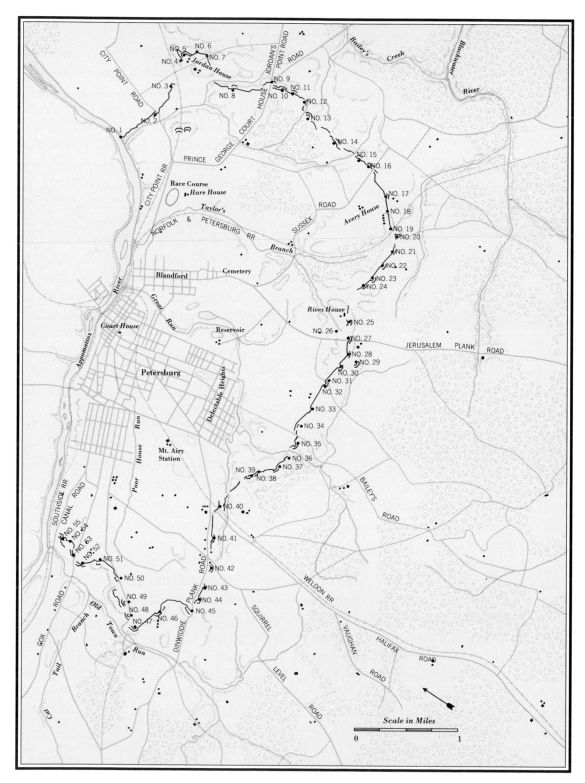

The defense of Petersburg by General Pierre Gustave Toutant Beauregard (*right*) was bold and brilliant. By counterattacking at intervals, he deluded the Federals into thinking his thinly spread force was stronger than it really was; he was then able to withdraw to a more defensible line to await the arrival of reinforcements.

As a railroad hub linking Richmond with the Deep South, Petersburg was indispensable to the defense of the Confederate capital and the supply of Lee's army. This map shows the fortifications that ringed the city when the Federals attacked on June 15, 1864. Although Redans 4, 12, 13 and 14 fell quickly, the Confederates later erected a second line of works that would hold off the Union forces for another 10 months.

Beauregard knew better, for by 10 a.m. the skirmishing on Wise's front had assumed what he thought to be "alarming proportions." The order went out to Wise: "Hold on at all hazards!" Major General Robert Hoke's division, dispatched earlier by General Lee, was on its way to Petersburg.

By noon Kautz had reached the Norfolk & Petersburg in the vicinity of Redan No. 20 on Wise's right. There he encountered Brigadier General James Dearing with a battery and two small regiments of dismounted Confederate cavalry, no more than 600 men in all. Though heavily outnumbered, Dearing held his ground for some time.

After skirmishing for another two hours under heavy artillery fire from the enemy redans, Kautz decided to attack the thinly defended works. But he got no closer than 500 yards before he became convinced that "our line was really weaker than the enemy's in men." Kautz dawdled for another two hours, listening for the sound of Smith's attack to his right. Then, in a replay of the June 9 fiasco, Kautz gave up and withdrew.

Smith, meanwhile, had been conducting what Butler would later scorn as "interminable reconnaissances." Butler was no professional soldier, but here, at least, he hit the mark. Smith, whose corps had been decimated in the disastrous Cold Harbor assaults of June 3, knew what it meant to attack well-manned fortifications across open ground. That knowledge undoubtedly made him cautious as he drove in the skirmishers and approached the main Confederate defenses around 1:30 p.m. Then he stopped and spent the next five and a half hours making an extensive survey of the situation.

Smith faced an open stretch of ground swept by concentrated artillery fire from the

Confederate redans. Although he suspected the fortifications were only lightly supported by infantry, he concluded that it would be suicidal to attack in columns against such cannon fire. Instead, he decided to mass his own artillery and fire against one of the redans, then attack with a reinforced line of skirmishers. Such a spread-out formation would have a better chance of surviving the enemy shellfire and still provide enough troops to sweep out the defenders.

But then the hapless Smith found that Colonel Henry Burton, his artillery commander, without authority and contrary to basic military sense, had decided to water all the artillery horses at the same time. Smith's guns were thus immobilized for a full hour.

Finally, at 7 p.m. — more than two hours after Kautz had fallen back — Smith ordered his corps to move against Redans Nos. 5, 6 and 7, while Hinks's division attacked on the left as far down as Redan No. 11.

By this time, General Beauregard had arrived to take charge of the defense. He wrote

later that "thinned out and exhausted as they were, Wise's heroic forces resisted still." But when the Federal infantry, 14,000 strong, smashed into the fortifications held by roughly 2,000 infantry and militiamen, a mile-wide section of the Confederate line gave way. From Redans 3 to 11, Smith's attacking force rolled into and over Beaure-

Pieced together, the sketches below by newspaper artist Edwin Forbes give a panoramic view of the outer Confederate works at Petersburg, built by Captain Charles H. Dimmock (*left*). Dimmock's line, which Forbes identified by the number *2*, is visible just in front of the treeline. Attacking Federal troops are identified by the numbers *8* (Hancock's II Corps) and *9* (Smith's XVIII Corps).

gard's works. Hinks's black infantrymen distinguished themselves by capturing seven Confederate guns.

The road into Petersburg lay open. Beauregard wrote later that the city "at that hour was clearly at the mercy of the Federal commander, who had all but captured it." Yet Smith stopped. He reported the next day, "Deeming that I held important points of the enemy's line of works, I thought it prudent to make no farther advance." One cause of his excessive wariness was a rumor that reinforcements were coming into the city; the rumor started with the arrival of Hoke's division, which went into line behind the works just taken by the Federals.

Even now the capable General Hancock might have saved the situation for the Federals, but command fumbles and sloppy communications conspired against him. Either Grant or Meade had failed to tell Hancock what he was expected to do that day beyond crossing the river and waiting to be resup-

plied. His men were famished. Rations that were being forwarded to his command had failed to arrive, and one soldier in the 4th New York Heavy Artillery grumbled that he was so hungry he "could eat a raw dog with the hair on." Moreover, Hancock had been instructed to halt at a place on the way to Petersburg that did not exist. At 5:30 p.m. he was wandering the countryside, trying to find where he was supposed to be, when he received a dispatch from Grant directing him to hurry and support Smith in the attack on Petersburg. Hancock insisted later that this was the first indication he had received that any attack was planned for that day.

Completing a four-mile march, Hancock had arrived on the scene shortly after the Confederate line had given way. Though senior to Smith, Hancock at once offered to accept his judgment on whether or not to renew the attack, and Smith demurred. Much later, when it had become obvious that this was the wrong decision, Smith would try

to suggest that the error was Hancock's, for being late and for not insisting on the assault.

Hancock, still suffering from a severe wound received at Gettysburg, and no doubt frustrated by the lost opportunity, went to the rear and vented his anger by upbraiding one of his division commanders, Brigadier General John Gibbon, for a slight infraction of marching procedure. That evening the moon over Petersburg rose nearly full; it was, as one of Hancock's artillerymen declared, a night "made to fight on." Nevertheless, Smith could not bring himself to risk a night assault, and the moment passed.

That was the end of Smith's career. He continued in charge of his corps for a month but was relieved in July and would hold no further field command during the War.

The sorry performance of the Federal commanders in front of Petersburg stood in stark contrast to that of the senior Confederate officer, General Beauregard. A contentious and supremely self-confident man, he was an occasionally brilliant commander. And he never served the Confederacy better than in these June days when, almost alone in the high command, he perceived, and opposed, the threat to Petersburg and to Lee.

Beauregard worked feverishly all night on June 15, supervising the building of new entrenchments for Hoke's men and repositioning the remnants of Wise's command. He sent a flurry of telegrams to the War Department in Richmond and to Lee, warning of the emergency and asking for reinforcements. His small contingent could not defend both his Bermuda Hundred line and the city, Beauregard said; and he asked Richmond which was more important. Receiving no answer, he made the decision himself and ordered the division under Major General Bushrod Johnson, the only one still facing Butler at Bermuda Hundred, to pull out and march to Petersburg with all speed.

As it turned out, several of Beauregard's messages were not relayed to Lee but were simply filed. Thus at 2 a.m. on June 16, when Lee learned that Beauregard had evacuated Johnson's division, he could not fully understand why. He knew by this time that Smith's corps had returned to Butler and that the Federals on Bermuda Hundred intended to give trouble. But he had no evidence that the Army of the Potomac had crossed the James, and until its location was verified he did not dare uncover Richmond's eastern defenses.

Beauregard's news worried him enough to temporize, however. He would move his headquarters south of the river and would take with him two divisions from Lieutenant General Richard Anderson's corps to hold the Bermuda Hundred line. Anderson's 3rd Division, along with all of Lieutenant General A. P. Hill's corps, would remain in place east of Richmond.

It would take Lee 24 hours to reach Johnson's empty lines; in that time Butler could have marched to the Richmond & Petersburg Railroad, in Beauregard's rear and between Beauregard and Lee, with virtually no opposition. Characteristically, Butler would not take the chance, even when he knew that Grant was sending him General Wright with two divisions of VI Corps to help out.

By dawn on June 16, Beauregard had concentrated about 14,000 men in a bent but shored-up line east of Petersburg. That represented a vast improvement over the previous day, but before many hours had passed, the Confederates once again were facing an overwhelmingly superior force.

Late that morning Grant arrived with Burnside's IX Corps. Now there were about 50,000 Federals facing Petersburg.

Grant had spent a difficult day on the 15th, trying to find out what was happening to Smith's attack. He discovered the confusion in the orders for Hancock too late to remedy the failure. On arriving at the front the next morning, Grant ordered a reconnaissance to feel for weak points in the defenses. Hancock, in command until Meade was able to get there, massed Smith's XVIII Corps on the right, opposite Hoke in the first three redans and the new breastworks. Hancock took the center with II Corps, and Burnside's newly arrived IX Corps filed in on the left. Facing them was Bushrod Johnson's division in its hastily built defenses. Grant scheduled an assault for 6 p.m.

That morning, Beauregard learned of the presence of Hancock's corps from a prisoner. He implored Lee, "Could we not have more reinforcements here?" Lee apparently did not accept Beauregard's conclusion, if in fact he ever received the message; at 4 p.m. he wired Beauregard to ask, "Has Grant been seen crossing James River?" And three hours later Lee informed President Jefferson Davis that Beauregard was hard pressed in Petersburg but added, "I have not learned from General Beauregard what force is opposed to him. Nor have I been able to learn whether any portion of Grant's army is opposed to him." Yet, at that moment fully half of the Army of the Potomac was forcing Beauregard into a battle for his life.

It was about 5:30 p.m. when Hancock's II Corps, supported by elements of the two corps on his flanks, moved forward. Hancock's old Gettysburg wound had begun

suppurating and was causing him great pain. That morning, Colonel Thomas Egan's brigade had carried Redan No. 12; but now Hancock's units were slow to advance. Beauregard fought superbly, throwing up new breastworks in the rear of the breached line and continuing the resistance.

It was late in the day before Hancock and the newly arrived Meade got the attack going again. With a wave of his hat, Brigadier General Francis Barlow led his division against Redans 13, 14 and 15. Well-aimed Confederate artillery fire cut down scores of Federals — among the killed was Colonel Patrick Kelly, commander of the famed Irish Brigade — but Barlow managed to fight his way into the defenses.

His men could do no more. Exhausted by days and nights of marching, shaken by the stubborn resistance, they gave way before a determined counterattack. The 44th Tennessee alone captured nearly 200 Federals and the flag of the 7th New York Heavy Artillery. With night coming soon, Hancock's soldiers dug in close to the enemy works. "The men were utterly used up," reported Captain James Fleming of the 28th Massachusetts, "and dropped asleep in the pits."

On the left of the Federal line, Brigadier General Robert B. Potter spent the night getting two IX Corps brigades into position for a dawn attack. Under cover of darkness they crept down into a steep ravine tangled with felled trees. "We were so near the enemy," Brigadier General Simon Griffin wrote later, "that all our movements had to be made with the utmost care and caution; canteens were placed in knapsacks to prevent rattling, and all commands were given in whispers."

With the enemy fortifications looming over them a mere hundred yards away, the

Lieutenant Lucius G. Rees of Ross's Georgia Battery, described by his commander as a "gallant and meritorious officer," was killed by Federal artillery fire on June 20, 1864, while his battalion shelled the lines from the north side of the Appomattox.

men silently formed two lines. Just as dawn began to break on June 17, Potter gave the command: "Forward." "The men rose in a body from the ground," recalled Private Henry Rowe of the 11th New Hampshire. "Not a gunlock clicked; the bayonet was to do the work."

Surprise was complete. The startled defenders awoke to cries of "Surrender, you damned Rebels!" Nearly a mile of the Confederate fortifications fell to the Federals in minutes, along with four guns, five flags, 600 prisoners and 1,500 stands of arms. But the success was limited. Potter's men pushed forward until they came up against another entrenched line and were forced to halt. Because of the tangled logs in the ravine behind them, which could be swept by enfilading artillery fire from Confederate guns farther to the left, Federal attempts to support and enlarge upon Potter's breakthrough failed.

At 2 p.m. Burnside's corps mounted another attack, spearheaded by Brigadier General John F. Hartranft's brigade. In an error all too typical of the Federal high command that day, Hartranft's men were sent forward at a right angle to the Confederate works, which made them desperately vulnerable. Hartranft's division commander, Brigadier General Orlando Willcox, reported later that the brigade "melted out of sight" beneath the enfilading musketry and artillery fire. Just before sunset Brigadier General James Ledlie's division advanced, only to meet with a similar fate. Federal gains were small, the sacrifice great. Ledlie was visibly intoxicated, and one of his aides, Captain Charles J. Mills, commented that "the deep sense of mismanagement and waste of life were almost enough to drive us to despair."

Elsewhere along his line, Beauregard had

Officers and men of Captain Andrew Cowan's New York battery occupy Redan No. 5 (below), a strong point in the Dimmock Line captured on the evening of June 15. When the battery fell, Captain Nathaniel Sturdivant (inset), commander of the Albemarle Battery, Virginia Light Artillery, was taken prisoner by the Federals.

managed to repel most of the Federal advances, thanks in part to the fact that the attacks were uncoordinated. But he knew that he could not last much longer. During the day he had his chief engineer lay out a new defensive line nearly a mile behind the Dimmock redans, beyond the tracks of the Norfolk & Petersburg Railroad.

The new line ran along a marshy creek called Taylor's Branch from Redan No. 24 — which was south of the city, near the Jerusalem Plank Road — north to the Appomattox less than a mile from the city limits. Although the order to hold on at any cost remained in effect on the front, Beauregard had the new line marked with white stakes so that it could be seen in the moonlight, and he made sure that the staff officers of Hoke's and Johnson's divisions were shown where their places were to be.

As the firing continued after dark, Beauregard ordered campfires to be built high to make it appear that his command would hold its position. After placing sentinels far forward to provide a measure of cover, he pulled his men back at 12:30 a.m. on June 18 and posted them in the new line.

There was to be no rest for the Confederate soldiers, however, for now in the moonlight they commenced digging new defensive works and trenches. The men worked with axes, spades, knives and bayonets; some even used spoons and tin cans. Hundreds of slaves were also put to work digging. Beauregard's situation was desperate, and he no longer expected help from Lee's army. "I had failed to convince its distinguished commander," he wrote years later, with a remaining trace of bitterness, "of the fact that I was then fighting Grant's whole army."

In reality, however, Lee had become convinced of the truth earlier that afternoon. All day on the 16th and 17th, while his men sparred inconclusively with Butler's force on Bermuda Hundred, Lee had continued to sniff the wind for a sign of Grant's intentions. He had shifted more and more of his strength across the James, keeping his army balanced to move either north or south to meet the anticipated Federal thrust. Again and again, he demanded evidence of the whereabouts of the Army of the Potomac. From long experience he discounted strategic estimates of captured privates — and alarms raised by General Beauregard.

In the end it was not Beauregard, but the commanding general's son, Major General W.H.F. (Rooney) Lee, who provided the necessary evidence. His cavalry had patched together reliable reports of the pontoon bridge's existence and of Grant's crossing. Now at last the senior Lee moved with characteristic vigor, setting his entire army in motion for Petersburg.

As always, Lee's troops were confident; but they were suffering from the effects of six weeks' strenuous campaigning. "Our health was very bad," noted Lieutenant James F. J. Caldwell of the 1st South Carolina in a litany of complaint. "The constant exposure to sun and rain, the rancid bacon and half-raw cornbread that were issued us, the filth accompanying the scarcity of clothing, and the lack of opportunity for bathing or washing our clothes, the vile water of this section of the country, the want of rest at night, and the constant, excited anxiety, had produced and aggravated diarrhoea, dysentery, dyspepsia, and slow fevers, which were wasting men surely away."

Lee's march began at 3 a.m. on June 18, and at first light his two leading divisions filed in behind Beauregard's utterly exhausted troops, lying in despair in their scratched-out trenches. While Major General J. B. Kershaw's division relieved Bushrod Johnson's and Major General C. W. Field's extended the line to the right, Beauregard's battered veterans wept and cheered with joy.

By full daylight, Beauregard had 20,000 men under his command. But with the arrival of Warren's V Corps the previous afternoon, Grant now had 67,000 men present for duty, and the Confederates were barely in place when the Federals attacked.

Though superior in number, the Northern forces too were physically exhausted, and memories of the carnage in the Wilderness, at Spotsylvania and at Cold Harbor haunted their minds. Generals were no more immune to fatigue than privates, and from the onset of the assault on June 18 it became clear that a breakdown in leadership had occurred. Both Grant and Meade seemed strangely detached from the tactical reality of the situation, leaving the responsibility of the attack to their corps commanders. The result was a series of disjointed charges that failed — at great cost of life.

The initial attack was launched at dawn by II and XVIII Corps on the Federal right, although IX Corps in the center and V Corps on the left had greater distances to cover and should logically have moved out first. Through the early-morning hours Hancock had sent repeated messages urging Burnside to advance, but to no avail. In exasperation he exclaimed to his staff, "Gentlemen, poor old Burnside is so slow!" Shortly thereafter the wound in Hancock's thigh began to hem-

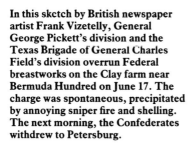

In this sketch by British newspaper artist Frank Vizetelly, General George Pickett's division and the Texas Brigade of General Charles Field's division overrun Federal breastworks on the Clay farm near Bermuda Hundred on June 17. The charge was spontaneous, precipitated by annoying sniper fire and shelling. The next morning, the Confederates withdrew to Petersburg.

orrhage, expelling several splinters of bone, and his staff surgeon ordered him to bed. Major General David B. Birney took command of II Corps.

Swarming into the works that had been held by the enemy the previous evening, Birney's Federals were startled by the lack of resistance. Slow to realize what had happened, they took too long to push back the Confederate skirmishers; when they came up against Beauregard's new line, their attack ground to a halt.

"Every step we advanced, the greater the slaughter," wrote Colonel Robert McAllister, who led a brigade in Gershom Mott's division of II Corps. "Advance — we could not live; retreat — we would not without orders; and every regimental flag was planted in line of battle over the living and the dead, my command lying flat on the ground, waiting for orders, with flags to the breeze." McAllister protested to his superiors that the position was a "death trap," but he was told to resist until Burnside and Warren arrived.

It was noon before IX and V Corps came abreast of Birney's men. By then most of II Corps had been under fire for eight hours, and losses had been high. Again the men rose to attack. "I shall never forget the hurricane of shot and shell which struck us as we emerged from the trees," recalled Captain A. C. Brown of the 4th New York Heavy Artillery. "The sound of the whizzing bullets and exploding shells, blending in awful volume, seemed like the terrific hissing of some gigantic furnace. Men, torn and bleeding, fell headlong from the ranks as the murderous hail swept through the line. The shrieks of the wounded mingled with the shouts of defiance which greeted us as we neared the rebel works."

Burnside's subsequent attack fared little better than Birney's. With Willcox's division in the lead, the Federals occupied the abandoned Confederate line and pushed on, to a deep cut made by the tracks of the Norfolk & Petersburg Railroad. There Willcox halted while Burnside's other divisions came up and V Corps advanced on the left. The men dug toeholds in the nearly perpendicular face of the railroad embankment, and when orders came to renew the attack they scrambled out into an open field crossed by Taylor's Branch. In the marsh, the charge dissolved in the fire that poured from Beauregard's defenses. Within minutes one of Willcox's brigades lost three commanders in succession, and several regiments took casualties of 50 percent or more. By the end of the day Willcox could muster only 1,000 men — the regulation strength of a single regiment.

On Burnside's left, some regiments of Warren's V Corps also reached Taylor's Branch, at the point where it flowed through a narrow ravine. But it soon became obvious that to advance any farther was suicidal. Ahead lay a formidable Confederate earthwork known as Rives's Salient, which spewed death into the ranks of the Federal attackers. "It was beyond human endurance to stand such an iron hail without stronger supports," wrote Robert G. Carter of the 22nd Massachusetts. "Our men broke and came back, a bleeding, routed body of men." Though only a private, Carter saw all too clearly the reason for failure: "There seemed to be no concerted movement at all."

At Union headquarters the tension was exacerbated by a growing sense of frustration and anger. "Everyone was near the breaking-point," noted Meade's aide, Colonel Theodore Lyman. Late in the afternoon

A Union Hero's Miraculous Recovery

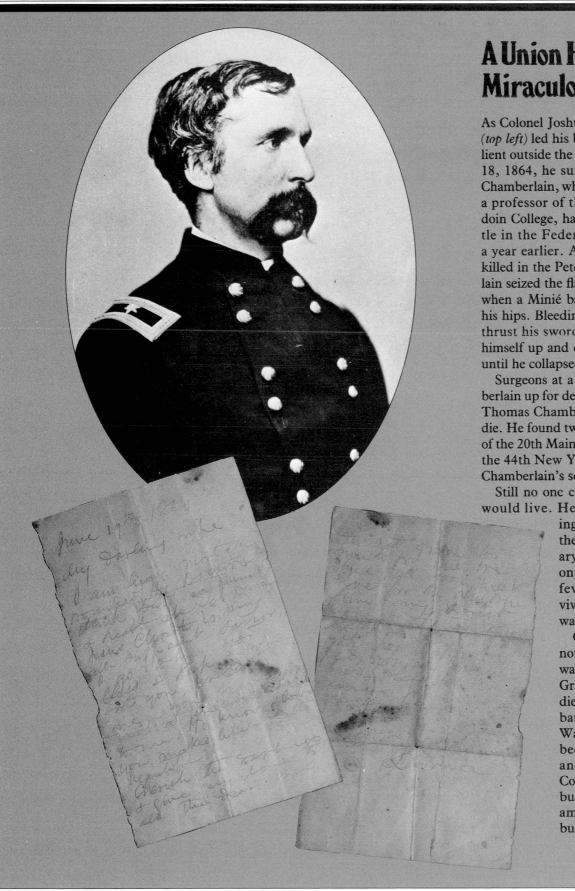

As Colonel Joshua Lawrence Chamberlain *(top left)* led his brigade against Rives's Salient outside the city of Petersburg on June 18, 1864, he suffered a grievous wound. Chamberlain, who before the War had been a professor of theology at Maine's Bowdoin College, had already proved his mettle in the Federal victory at Gettysburg a year earlier. After his color-bearer was killed in the Petersburg assault, Chamberlain seized the flag and was holding it aloft when a Minié ball slammed through both his hips. Bleeding profusely, Chamberlain thrust his sword into the ground to prop himself up and continued shouting orders until he collapsed.

Surgeons at a field hospital gave Chamberlain up for dead. But his brother, Major Thomas Chamberlain, refused to let him die. He found two physicians, Abner Shaw of the 20th Maine and M. W. Townsend of the 44th New York, who pieced together Chamberlain's severed tissue.

Still no one expected that Chamberlain would live. He wrote his wife a touching farewell note *(left),* and the Army released his obituary. For weeks he lay in agony, racked with chills and fever. Not only did he survive, but five months later he was back in combat.

Chamberlain's bravery had not gone unnoticed. Without waiting for approval, General Grant promoted him to brigadier general — the only such battlefield promotion of the War. Chamberlain went on to become Governor of Maine and President of Bowdoin College. Returning to Petersburg years later, he mused: "I am not of Virginia's blood, but she is of mine."

Meade ordered another headlong assault, but it met with the same fate as the others. "The men went in, but not with spirit," Lyman recalled. "Received by a withering fire, they sullenly fell back a few paces to a slight crest and lay down, as much to say, 'We can't assault but we won't run.' " It was sadly apparent, Lyman concluded, that "you cannot strike a full blow with a wounded hand."

During this assault, the greatest slaughter of the day occurred. In the forefront of the Federal attack marched the 900 men of the 1st Maine Heavy Artillery, a regiment only recently arrived from the defenses of Washington and assigned to duty as infantry. The regiment's division commander, General Mott, watched the troops march forward "like a blue wave crested with a glistening foam of steel." Within minutes, however,

their enthusiastic cheers gave way to the screams of the wounded and dying. The 1st Maine lost 632 men, the heaviest battle loss of any regiment during the entire War.

Lee had arrived in Petersburg around noon on the 18th, with the fighting well under way. Beauregard immediately took his chief to the city reservoir, on an eminence with a broad view of Petersburg, and from it pointed out the prominent features of the field, his defenses and troop positions. Then, ever the grand planner, Beauregard proposed that after the balance of the army had arrived, they should move out and strike Grant's left and rear and attempt to drive the Federals back to the James before they could entrench. He argued that the enemy must be tired and depressed after four days of failure.

Brigadier General James H. Wilson (*reclining at center*) sits with his staff on the steps of a mansion at City Point, Virginia, after his Petersburg raid. When Grant gave Wilson, a 27-year-old former staff officer, command of the 3rd Cavalry Division, jealous senior officers claimed favoritism — a charge Wilson's capable performance swiftly laid to rest.

But Lee knew how tired his own army was. That afternoon, as A. P. Hill's corps marched through Petersburg, a resident of the city recognized some local boys; they were, she wrote in her diary, "so worn with travel and fighting, so dusty and ragged, their faces so thin and drawn with privation that we scarcely knew them." Lee's strategy all along had been to remain on the defensive; with his weary forces heavily outnumbered, this was no time to change.

By the end of the day Grant had gained little. The Confederates still held most of their new line, and evening attacks by parts of Burnside's and Warren's commands accomplished nothing further. Concluding "that all has been done that can be done," George Meade ordered the Federal commanders to dig in where they were.

But Lee and Beauregard knew how temporary a victory over General Grant could be. All night long they worked to shore up their lines. For once, however, the implacable Grant had had enough. After executing one of the most remarkable maneuvers of the War, his army had suffered more than 10,000 casualties in four days of fighting. "I have some grit left yet," wrote Private Carter of the 22nd Massachusetts, "although the greater part of it was frightened out of me yesterday afternoon." Carter and his comrades had not achieved anything conclusive, but they had inched the noose a little tighter around the neck of the Army of Northern Virginia. For the moment, Grant was content. He ordered Meade to "rest the men and use the shade for their protection until a new vein can be struck."

Grant did not want a siege, but the battle had proved unsuccessful. He had been through one siege already in this war, at Vicksburg. It had lasted 47 tedious days, and the inactivity had made it difficult to maintain discipline and morale in the ranks. Lee was stronger than Lieutenant General John C. Pemberton had been, and Petersburg was better defended, with several supply routes still open. A siege here would last much longer than at Vicksburg and would be more stubbornly contested. Nevertheless, on June 20 Grant told Butler and others, "I have determined to try to envelop Petersburg."

That same day he also set in motion one last attempt to force Lee out in the open. His army now lay across the Norfolk & Petersburg Railroad east of the city and was in striking distance of two more of Lee's remaining sources of supply: the Weldon Railroad, which ran into North Carolina and on to the port of Wilmington, and the Southside Railroad, running west to Lynchburg. If he could cut these lines, even temporarily, Lee might be forced to attack him or to abandon Richmond and Petersburg altogether.

Grant ordered General Wilson to take his own cavalry division and Kautz's on a wide sweeping ride around the enemy right. Grant wanted Wilson to cross the Weldon line as close to Petersburg as possible, cut it, then ride on to the Southside, once again as close to the city as practicable. Then he was to tear up track as far west as he could get, if possible the entire 45 miles to Burke's Station, where the Southside intersected with the Richmond & Danville line.

From there, if still unmolested, Wilson and Kautz were to continue the destruction, moving southwest on the Richmond & Danville. If they were successful, only one line — the Virginia Central — would be left intact to serve the Army of Northern Virginia.

Grant expected that Sheridan, who was on

Destruction of Genl. Lees lines of communication in Virginia

Units of Brigadier General James H. Wilson's cavalry rip up and burn railroad ties on the Southside Railroad west of Petersburg. "The hot weather favored us," Wilson recalled. "It made buildings, crossties, trestles, wood piles, cars and stations so dry and inflammable that they burned like tinder, filling the air with clouds of cinders and smoke."

his way back east from the Trevilian raid, would keep most of Wade Hampton's cavalry occupied, though Rooney Lee's mounted division would have to be dealt with. As further cover for the movement, Grant ordered Birney and Wright to move to their left, across the Jerusalem Plank Road and out to the Weldon line in the vicinity of Globe Tavern. They might do considerable damage to the railroad themselves, and they would also provide a screen behind which Wilson could get well on his way.

Wilson asked for two days to rest and refit his men. Then, before dawn on June 22, he set out with a total of about 5,000 troopers. By midmorning they had reached Reams's Station on the Weldon line without opposition; they stopped briefly to burn the railroad buildings and uproot the tracks for a few hundred yards on either side. That done, the raiders moved on, and by afternoon they passed through Dinwiddie Court House, with Rooney Lee now sniping ineffectually at their heels.

Before nightfall Wilson and Kautz reached Ford's Station on the Southside line, where they had the good fortune to find two loaded enemy supply trains. These they burned, along with the station buildings and everything else combustible. Then they headed west, tearing up the track as they went, heating it red-hot over fires fed with railroad ties and then twisting the rails out of shape to render them useless. Not until midnight did the Federal raiders finally halt, more than 50 miles from their starting point. The exhausted men slept with their reins in their hands, lying in formation in front of their saddled horses.

The following morning, while Kautz's men rode ahead toward the Richmond &

Danville line, Wilson's men continued their work, moving slowly west while Rooney Lee's cavalry skirmished in their rear. "We had no time to do a right job," a trooper complained. Now they simply overturned the rails and ties, which could be done quickly but was hardly a permanent form of destruction. The next day they reached Burke's Station and met Kautz, who had reduced the depot to a charred ruin and had torn up the Richmond & Danville line for several miles in either direction.

Kautz took the advance again and headed out, reaching the Staunton River 30 miles southwest of Burke's Station on the afternoon of June 25. Destruction of the bridge here would be a hard blow to the Confederates, but by now the raiders were expected. More than 1,000 home guards, supported by at least one battery, waited in earthworks on the far side of the river. When Kautz advanced to burn the bridge, the defenders opened a stubborn fire and drove the Federals back. At the same time, Rooney Lee was pressing Wilson's rear guard. Wilson decided it was time to end the raid and return to friendly lines.

For several reasons, this was not going to be easy. Wilson was 100 miles from safety, with tired animals and worn-out men. General Hampton was on his way back to the Petersburg area with his two divisions of Confederate cavalry. And friendly lines were not where Wilson thought they were. Wright and Birney had moved their corps as ordered on June 22, but they had become separated in the woods, and A. P. Hill's Confederates had shoved their way between them. Hill stopped Wright short and forced the Federals back. Then he struck Birney ferociously and threw him back to the Jerusalem Plank Road, taking 1,700 prisoners. As a result, the Weldon Railroad was still firmly in Confederate hands.

At midday on June 28, Wilson's weary riders reached Stony Creek Depot, just 10 miles south of Reams's Station, and presumed safety. But here they ran into Wade Hampton's and Fitzhugh Lee's cavalry divisions. The dismayed Wilson could not break through; his line of retreat was cut off and he was in real trouble.

That night Wilson ordered Kautz to ride west and north, around the enemy divisions to Reams's Station; Wilson would hold Hampton at Stony Creek. While Wilson fought off a substantial attack, Kautz reached Reams's Station the next day — only to discover, instead of the Federal II and VI Corps, part of Fitzhugh Lee's cavalry and two brigades of Hill's Confederate infantry.

Increasingly desperate, Wilson next took his own command around the opponents facing him to rejoin Kautz west of Reams's Station. But now the enemy was converging on him from three sides: Fitzhugh and Rooney Lee's cavalrymen from the north, Hill's infantry from the east, and Hampton's riders from the south. There was no choice but to make a headlong run for it.

The Federals burned their wagons, spiked their guns, left their wounded behind and headed southwest. Before they could get away, the Confederates attacked and Kautz, in covering the escape of Wilson, became separated from him.

There was a large swamp on the enemy left flank, and Kautz thought he saw a chance to break through there. "It was our only chance," wrote one of his troopers. In they plunged, the men riding past Kautz, who was sitting astride his horse, one leg slung over his pommel, with a pocket map of Virginia in one hand and a compass in the other. Looking at the sun for position, he pointed out their course. Incredibly, the troopers got through the swamp unopposed. Seven hours later, bone-weary and falling asleep in their saddles, they rode into friendly lines southeast of Petersburg.

Wilson's men had it even tougher. For 11 hours they were pursued south, until they were nearly 20 miles farther away from Federal lines. Wilson allowed the men two hours' rest, then he led them east, toward the James River. Riding all day June 30, with Hampton racing to cut them off, the Federals finally reached Blackwater River — seven miles south of the James — after midnight, on July 1.

There was no enemy on the other side of Blackwater River, but Wilson found the only bridge burned. Hastily the troopers made makeshift repairs and straggled across; that afternoon they reached the James and safety, having covered 125 miles in 60 hours. "For the first time in ten days," Wilson wrote later, his men "unsaddled, picketed, fed, and went regularly to sleep."

Like most cavalry raids in this War, Wilson's had been audacious, dramatic — and

Bone-tired after a week of riding, ripping up railroad track and fighting off the enemy, General August Kautz's cavalry division plods toward the Federal lines near Petersburg. In the foreground, a runaway slave who has joined the raiders assists a trooper who has lost his mount.

had yielded mixed results. Undeniably the destruction of more than 60 miles of railroad track was important. Years later Colonel Isaac M. St. John, who was in charge of Confederate ordnance supplies in Richmond, said that nine weeks passed before another train entered either Petersburg on the Southside Railroad or Richmond on the Richmond & Danville. The ensuing shortages forced Lee's army to consume every bit of its commissary reserves, yet it was not forced out of Petersburg, much less Richmond. Meanwhile, Wilson had lost all of his artillery, wagons and supplies, along with one quarter of his command in casualties.

It seemed to many that for all the sweat and blood, Grant had accomplished very little; Richmond, Petersburg and the Shenan-doah Valley all remained in enemy hands, and the Army of the Potomac was no closer to Richmond than it had been after Cold Harbor. But Grant knew better. Although he would have to adopt siege tactics, and as he told Halleck, such tactics would be tedious, the outcome was certain. "Be of good cheer," he wrote to a friend in Chicago, "and rest assured that all will come out right."

One other person who understood what Grant had achieved was Robert E. Lee. The master of maneuver now found himself immobilized, in a situation he had been dreading. "We must destroy this army of Grant's before he gets to the James River," he had told Jubal Early weeks before. "If he gets there it will become a siege, and then it will be a mere question of time."

This swallow-tailed guidon was carried as a flank marker by a company in the 1st Maine. Like other heavy artillery regiments, the 1st Maine was organized into 12 companies of 150 men each, rather than into the infantry's 10 companies of 100 men.

Halcyon Days of an Ill-fated Regiment

The 18th Maine was one of many volunteer regiments that flocked to the Union colors in the summer of 1862. The enlistees were a hardy lot: sailors and fishermen from Maine's rugged coast, farmers and lumbermen from the Penobscot River valley. On August 21 they were mustered into service at Bangor, and after getting uniforms and Enfield rifles, they traveled by rail to Washington, D.C., eager to fight. Instead, the regiment was assigned to nearly two years of garrison duty in the capital. As Private Thomas Libby lamented, "Drilling, building forts, felling trees, picket and guard duty was our daily life."

Eventually the 18th became proficient at operating the cannon that defended the city, and the regiment was reorganized as the 1st Maine Heavy Artillery. Then, in the spring of 1864, General Grant needed infantry reinforcements for his Virginia Campaign. The New Englanders, polished but still unblooded, left their big guns and comfortable quarters behind and marched to their belated appointment with war.

A detachment of the 1st Maine drills in Fort Sumner, Maryland, during the winter of 1863. Fort Sumner, the regiment's regular station, was built on a bluff that overlooked the Potomac on the northwestern rim of Washington's defenses.

Musicians of the 1st Maine's regimental band gather in front of Oak Hill, a plantation house next to Fort Sumner. During their long Washington sojourn, the band members practiced daily in the woods behind the house.

Although the men of the 1st Maine were armed and equipped as infantry, they wore the regulation uniform of the Federal artillery — a red-trimmed frock coat *(left)* and forage cap with crossed-cannon insignia *(below)*.

The sketch below shows the Union right wing moving forward from abandoned Confederate earthworks toward Petersburg *(background)* early on June 18, 1864. Later that day the 1st Maine Heavy Artillery advanced across the field to attack entrenched Confederates near the Hare house, visible atop the hill at left.

Petersburg

captured Confederate works —

Confederate bork

18th Corps

union infantry 18th Corps

The siege of Petersburg Va — advance of the Union on the right near the Appomattox showing the captured works and the part of the city

E Forbes —

It was said of Colonel Daniel Chaplin *(right)*, commander of the 1st Maine: "His presence carried authority which no one questioned." Chaplin survived the June 18 charge at Petersburg, but two months later he was killed by a sharpshooter's bullet. "There was not a dry eye in the regiment," a grieving veteran wrote. "The boys cried like children."

Appomattox river

Union
line behind breastworks

ank.
Confederate fort.

Captured Confederate way

the morning of June 18th 1864
fire.

Ten Minutes of "Seething Hell"

SGT. MARK EMERSON (AND DAUGHTER)
Company F
Mortally wounded

On the afternoon of June 18, the 1st Maine Heavy Artillery spearheaded a desperate Federal charge on the Confederate works just east of Petersburg. "A shower of lead struck us," Corporal Charles House recalled. "The men involuntarily pulled their cap visors down over their eyes and advanced against the storm." Although the support troops behind them gave way, the artillerymen-turned-infantry pressed on. "The earth was literally torn with iron and lead," Lieutenant Horace Shaw remembered; "the field became a burning, seething, crashing, hissing hell."

After 10 minutes of slaughter, the survivors retreated to their starting point, leaving hundreds of stricken comrades behind. "The 1st Maine Heavy Artillery made for itself a record it did not seek," Lieutenant Shaw later wrote. Of the nearly 900 men who launched the charge, 632 were dead, wounded or missing — the greatest loss in battle of any Civil War regiment. Among the fallen were the men shown here.

LT. THOMAS DRUMMOND
Company D
Killed

LT. HUGH PORTER
Company K
Wounded

LT. ALBERT EASTMAN
Company M
Wounded

LT. ANDREW HILTON
Company B
Wounded

CAPT. WILLIAM PARKER
Company L
Killed

CAPT. ANDREW JAQUITH
Company I
Mortally wounded

LT. ALBERT ABBOTT
Company B
Killed

CAPT. FREDERIC HOWES
Company G
Killed

CAPT. WHITING CLARK
Company E
Wounded

LT. JAMES HALL
Company G
Killed

LT. CALVIN GARDNER
Company K
Wounded

LT. WILLIAM BECKFORD
Company D
Wounded

LT. WILLIAM NEWENHAM
Company H
Mortally wounded

LT. GARDNER RUGGLES
Company F
Killed

LT. GEORGE FERNALD
Company F
Wounded

LT. JOHN LANCY
Company F
Wounded

LT. HORATIO SPOONER
Company L
Mortally wounded

LT. ALLEN BARRY
Company H
Killed

LT. JAMES CLARK
Adjutant
Mortally wounded

MAJ. GEORGE SABINE
Mortally wounded

Valor and Calamity at the Crater

On the hot afternoon of June 30, 1864, Robert E. Lee took a rare moment away from his duties for personal reflection. He was in his headquarters — his usual, battered field tent, pitched in the backyard of a fine house on the north side of the Appomattox River, just across from Petersburg. Wearied by long and agonized effort, beleaguered by the unpredictable Ulysses S. Grant and his legions, the 57-year-old commanding general took out pen and paper and thought about his invalid wife, Mary, still in Richmond, their lost home and better times. It was the anniversary of their wedding.

"Do you recollect," he wrote to Mary, "what a happy day thirty-three years ago this was? How many hopes and pleasures it gave birth to?" As hard as it must have been to reflect on the course of events, Lee would not yield to even a hint of bitterness. "I pray that He may continue His mercies and blessings to us, and give us a little peace and rest together in this world."

Lee had scarcely finished writing when the burdens of the War came crashing in upon him once again. President Jefferson Davis had arrived from Richmond to discuss the military situation.

In a word, circumstances were grim, for both sides. Lee was pinned behind his fortifications by the need to defend his rail network. He was barely able to feed his men, and there was some doubt as to how rapidly and efficiently he could move if he wanted

to; lack of forage for his horses had necessitated their dispersal, and gathering them would require time.

Even Grant could no longer shrug off his casualties and press on. In addition to the men he had lost in combat, he had to watch several thousand experienced troops form up and march away North, their enlistment terms expired. Moreover, Jubal Early, with Lee's II Corps, not only had retaken the Shenandoah Valley but was driving north toward the Potomac, forcing the Federals to rush reinforcements to defend Washington.

The Army of the Potomac was hemorrhaging manpower, yet by mid-July it would still have almost 70,000 men facing Lee's 36,000 entrenched at Petersburg. At Bermuda Hundred and at Deep Bottom, a Federal bridgehead north of the James River, Butler's 40,000-man Army of the James faced 21,000 men in Lee's Richmond garrison.

The veterans who remained in the lines were suffering from severe combat fatigue, and their replacements had to be trained before they could fight. It was clear that both armies would have to be rested and rebuilt before they would be fit to make another assault of any kind. Thus the men put aside their muskets for a while, took up spades and began to dig. The Southerners dug because only massive fortifications could give them the edge they needed to resist the superior numbers of the Federals. The Northerners dug because only when their line was strong

This board, pried from a crate, served to mark the grave of Lieutenant George L. Vaughn of the 48th Georgia, who fell in the savage fighting that followed the explosion of the Federal mine near Petersburg on the morning of July 30, 1864. The marker was inscribed at the battle site by the lieutenant's brother.

enough to resist attack — even when lightly manned — could they dare to concentrate a force for an assault or a flanking movement.

On July 9, General George Meade issued an order that the campaign would progress by "regular approaches." The phrase meant traditional siege tactics — inching toward the enemy in trenches until his line could be cracked — although the Confederates were not surrounded and this was technically not a siege. The War had changed: Where there had been endless marching there was now perpetual digging. The men often turned out for duty at 4 a.m. and worked until evening, digging for two hours, then resting for two, through the blazing heat of the day.

Both sides dug far more than the usual Civil War breastworks, which consisted of a ditch with a raised earthen parapet fronted by abatis made of sharpened tree branches. At Petersburg they threw up enclosed redans or forts as strong points for infantry and artillery. They also scooped out additional trenches behind, and parallel to, the forward line and connected the lines with zigzagging communication trenches. Then they linked this labyrinth to the rear with covered ways — sunken roads along which men, guns and wagons could move under cover from enemy guns.

Normal field artillery with its flat trajec-

tory and relatively small projectiles could not do much damage to men in such burrows, but that soon changed. As early as April, Colonel Henry L. Abbot of the 1st Connecticut Heavy Artillery had been ordered to organize a siege train from his 1,700-man regiment. Once the Federal line stabilized in June, Abbot brought up his formidable train and emplaced 40 rifled siege guns and 60 mortars capable of lofting shells into the enemy trenches. The Confederates soon responded in kind, and the shelling became a daily, deadly factor in the life of the men, who immediately began constructing bomb-proofs with timber-and-sod roofs in addition to their other excavations.

Even the weather conspired to make life miserable. It had not rained since Cold Harbor; it had been hot; and now it became hotter than anyone could remember. Powdery dust, inches thick, covered everything, ready to well up in choking clouds at the slightest movement. Surface water virtually disappeared, providing yet another motive for digging; not far down, a substratum of clay held a ready supply of cool water.

Thus the days of July passed, with the sun burning down and the men hot, sweaty, filthy and frightened; with the musketry cracking along the trenches when any soldier showed himself to the enemy; and with the big guns and mortars thumping away.

The only exception to the general lassitude along the three-mile front was to be found among members of a single regiment at the center of the Federal line. These men made up the 48th Pennsylvania, part of Major General Ambrose Burnside's IX Corps. In peacetime they had been miners of anthracite in Schuylkill County, and they had come

up with a novel idea for striking a useful blow. No one among them suspected that their project would grow into one of the most macabre episodes in the annals of the War.

During the fighting of June 18, the 400 Pennsylvanians had pushed forward a little farther than the units on either side of them. They had crossed a deep ravine and had struggled up the slope on the opposite side to within 130 yards of the Confederate line. There, closer to the enemy than any other Federal unit, they dug in. Those who dared to peer over their parapets saw, on the crest of the rise, a redan containing Pegram's Richmond Battery and entrenchments stretching north and south. These were manned by South Carolina troops, part of a brigade commanded by Brigadier General Stephen Elliott Jr. of Bushrod Johnson's division. The redan and its supporting trenches came to be called Elliott's Salient.

The salient's location was critical to the Confederate defenses. About 500 yards beyond it the Jerusalem Plank Road ran north along another crest to Petersburg; a half mile to the northwest, on the outskirts of the city, rose an eminence called Cemetery Hill, which dominated the surrounding terrain, including Petersburg.

It was Lieutenant Colonel Henry Pleasants, in charge of the 48th Pennsylvania, who conceived the plan for destroying Elliott's Salient: His men would run a tunnel underneath the redan and blow it out of existence. Pleasants, who had been a mining engineer before the War, risked Confederate sniper fire to make careful observations of the enemy position. Then he took his audacious proposal to his division commander, Brigadier General Robert B. Potter, who forwarded it to General Burnside.

Ambrose Burnside's uneven and sometimes disastrous performance thus far in the War had not diminished his quick and unshakable enthusiasm. Burnside summoned Pleasants to his tent on the evening of June 24 to have the colonel explain the mining idea; he immediately approved the project and promised to get headquarters' support for it as soon as possible. Pleasants' Pennsylvanians began digging the next day.

But at headquarters, neither Meade nor Grant expressed much interest in the undertaking. The general in chief regarded it merely "as a means of keeping the men occupied." Meade said later that it was in the wrong place, an area held by strong enemy positions on either flank and the rear. Meade's chief engineer, Major James C. Duane, pronounced the idea "clap-trap and nonsense," avowing that "such a length of mine had never been excavated in military operations, and could not be."

As a result, Pleasants got little cooperation. Lumber for shoring the tunnel was not forthcoming, and the men had to scrounge for it, searching abandoned sawmills and tearing down an old bridge. No one would furnish them with wheelbarrows, so they made do with cracker boxes fitted with hickory handles. It took several days to get the surveying instrument Pleasants needed to calculate the length of the tunnel. "I found it impossible," he reported afterward, "to get any assistance from anybody."

Undeterred, the miners pushed on with their extraordinary project. They began the tunnel, or gallery, in the ravine behind their lines, protected from enemy observation. Working in shifts round the clock, they were soon burrowing 40 feet a day through sand and clay. But they would not be able to complete the job if Pleasants could not solve the problem of ventilation.

The gallery was a small one — five feet high, four feet wide at the bottom and only two feet wide at the top — and the longer it became, the more difficult it would be for the men in it to breathe. This was the reason a tunnel as long as this one had to be — 510.8 feet, by Pleasants' eventual calculation — had seldom been attempted.

The solution Pleasants devised was ingenious. About 100 feet into the mine, still behind Federal lines, he ran a vertical shaft to the surface. He placed an airtight door across the tunnel between the vertical shaft and the mine opening. Next he had the men construct a wooden duct, eight inches square, that extended from the mine face, where they were digging, through the bottom of the door. Then a large fire was built and kept burning under the vertical shaft.

This apparatus created the draft that was needed. Air heated by the fire billowed up the shaft and, since the main gallery was sealed by the door, sucked replacement air through the long wooden duct. The fresh air erupted from the end of the channel, right where the miners were working.

Day after day the Pennsylvanians kept up their backbreaking work. One man dug, hunched over in the cramped gallery, while others carried away debris. Dirt, sand and clay came out of the tunnel in a steady stream until the miners had excavated a small mountain of material — 18,000 cubic feet of it, by Pleasants' calculation. All of it had to be disposed of without drawing the enemy's attention, so the Pennsylvanians spread it carefully over the ravine behind their works.

Despite their precautions, it was only a few days before at least one Confederate grew suspicious. Brigadier General E. Porter Alexander, the Army of Northern Virginia's chief of ordnance, noticed that the firing of the Federal sharpshooters had become very heavy directly opposite Elliott's Salient but slackened noticeably on either side. "That indicated that some operation was going on," Alexander wrote later. And by June 30, he recalled, "I became satisfied that the activity was underground."

That same day, as Alexander was returning from his observations, a bullet from one of the telltale sharpshooters brought him down. He was sent home to Georgia to recuperate; but before leaving, he called on General Lee to relay his suspicions.

The military correspondent of the London *Times*, Francis Lawley, who was visiting Lee's headquarters, heard of Alexander's concern and declared that there was little to worry about. The longest such tunnel for military operations, he said, had been dug during the siege of Lucknow, in India, some years earlier, and at 400 feet the ventilation problem had made it impossible to dig farther. Nevertheless, Lee took the warning seriously enough to order countermining near Elliott's Salient.

Other Confederates did not take the threat seriously. The men joked that Grant, in frustration, was tunneling all the way into Petersburg. They told new recruits to listen for the sound of a Yankee train running underfoot and to look for the steam of its engine rising through the cobblestone streets.

Meanwhile, Lee's engineers dallied. It was July 15, two weeks after Alexander's warning, before orders finally went out to start the countermines — on either side of Elliott's Salient and at two other redans nearby. Every 15 minutes the workers were to stop digging and listen attentively. If they heard the sound of picks, a charge was to be detonated in the countermine to cave in the Federal gallery. But days passed, and the Confederates heard nothing.

The defenders took other steps to avoid a breach in the salient. Colonel D. B. Harris, Beauregard's chief engineer, laid out a series of batteries covering the rear of the salient and began a retrenchment — a covering trench for the main line — with a raised parapet, or cavalier, dominating Pegram's redan.

All this time, Generals Grant and Lee had been focusing on Jubal Early's Washington raid. Lee hoped that the threat to the Union capital would force Grant either to weaken his forces around Richmond or to launch a premature attack that could well turn into a reprise of the slaughter at Cold Harbor. But Grant simply sent VI Corps and diverted XIX Corps, which had just arrived at Fort Monroe from New Orleans, to block Early and push him back to the Shenandoah.

On July 25, while that chase was still going on, Grant decided it was time to "do something in the way of offensive movement" at Richmond. He told Meade to mount a diversion north of the James, "having for its real object the destruction of the railroad on that side." He wanted Hancock and two divisions of Sheridan's cavalry to cross at Deep Bottom, 10 miles southeast of Richmond. Once across, Sheridan would attack the city if an opportunity presented itself. Hancock, who despite constant pain from his wound had resumed command of II Corps in late June, was to advance on the Confederates at Chaffin's Bluff to prevent reinforcements from crossing the James to oppose Sheridan.

If a cavalry attack on Richmond seemed unlikely to succeed, Sheridan was to ride around the city to the north and west. He was to cut the Virginia Central and destroy it as far as the North Anna. This would stop the flow of supplies from the Shenandoah and would interfere with Early's return to Lee.

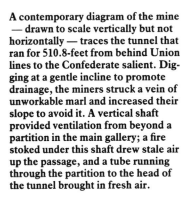

A contemporary diagram of the mine — drawn to scale vertically but not horizontally — traces the tunnel that ran for 510.8-feet from behind Union lines to the Confederate salient. Digging at a gentle incline to promote drainage, the miners struck a vein of unworkable marl and increased their slope to avoid it. A vertical shaft provided ventilation from beyond a partition in the main gallery; a fire stoked under this shaft drew stale air up the passage, and a tube running through the partition to the head of the tunnel brought in fresh air.

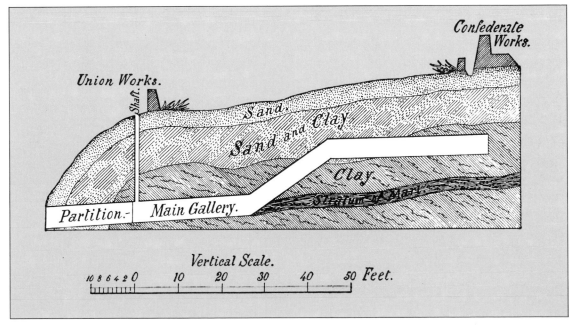

Meanwhile, Hancock just might find an opportunity for a grand stroke. "It is barely possible," Grant wrote, "that by a bold move this expedition may surprise the little garrison of citizen soldiery now in Richmond and get in." This was of course a long shot, but the threat alone might force Lee to shift a significant part of his army away from the defenses of Petersburg.

Grant told Meade exactly what to do if that happened: "Concentrate all the force possible at the point in the enemy's line we expect to penetrate." The attack must be made quickly, Grant said, and if it didn't succeed, must be abandoned just as quickly.

At 4 p.m. on July 26, Hancock's divisions began their nightlong journey northward, across both the Appomattox and the James. The march at first was uneventful; but at midmorning the next day, Hancock turned his men to the west and unexpectedly ran into a strongly fortified enemy line behind Bailey's Creek, which his advance had paralleled the day before.

Reports of Federal activity around Deep Bottom had alerted Lee to the possibility of Federal operations there. Four days earlier he had quietly begun pulling units out of the Petersburg line and sending them north until four full divisions were in place southeast of Richmond. On receiving word of Hancock's difficult situation, Grant was emphatic: "I do not want Hancock to attack intrenched lines." Instead, he directed that II Corps remain in place for another day while Sheridan's cavalry maneuvered to turn the Confederate left flank.

The cavalry fared little better. The troopers found the infantry division of Major General Joseph B. Kershaw posted squarely in their path on the New Market road. Ker-

Lieutenant Colonel Henry Pleasants of the 48th Pennsylvania, who oversaw the mining operation against Elliott's Salient, brought to the scheme the meticulous nature of a professional engineer and a venturesome streak that was part of his heritage. His father, a Philadelphia-bred arms merchant of Quaker stock, had smuggled guns to revolutionaries in Buenos Aires in the 1830s.

shaw attacked and drove Sheridan's lead brigade back, over the crest of a ridge. Here the Federal cavalrymen formed a battle line, dismounted and lay down on the ground. Kershaw's skirmishers stormed confidently over the crest — to confront a line of enemy carbines barely 15 yards away. A withering volley drove the Confederates back in disorder. Sheridan pursued with his mounted reserves, taking 250 prisoners and some battle flags, but in the presence of a large infantry force he dared not continue his raid.

"We have failed in what I had hoped to accomplish," Grant reported to Washington on July 28. And yet he had drawn four of Lee's divisions back to the north side of the James. That meant only three divisions, about 18,000 men, remained in the Petersburg works, and Meade should be ready to attack them. Thus, Grant ended his report, "I am yet in hopes of turning this diversion to account." The lightly regarded project of blowing up an enemy fort suddenly took on enormous importance.

For a few days after receiving Grant's directive to attack Petersburg, Meade

Three sketches detail the toils of Pleasants' Pennsylvanians. At top right, the lead miner swings his pick while others pack the soil in hardtack crates; at bottom left kegs of powder hidden in sandbags are hefted to the finished mine then placed in lateral shafts (bottom right) directly under the target. All this was carried out in sweltering heat, the artist noted, on ground "so slippery as to quickly tire anyone not used to such locomotion."

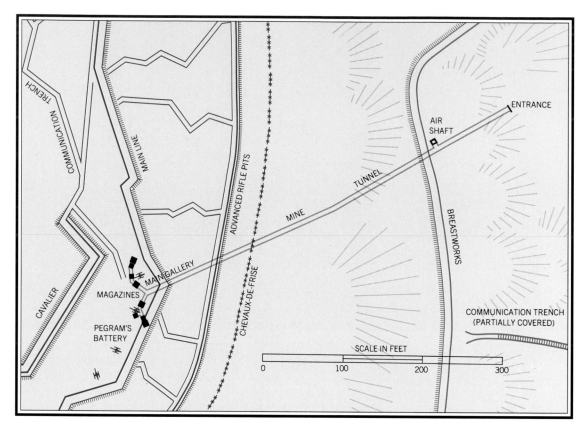

Once the miners had tunneled under the Confederate works, they branched out. To forge a wide breach in the enemy line, they extended two lateral shafts from the main gallery, which ended directly beneath William Pegram's battery. Each shaft housed four magazines that were stocked with black powder and linked to a single fuse.

had hemmed and hawed, contemplating the problems and polling his corps commanders for advice. On the 26th, Burnside submitted a plan: He would begin an assault by detonating Colonel Pleasants' mine — completed three days earlier — just before daylight. Then he would send two brigades in columns through the gap left by the explosion. A regiment at the head of one column would peel off to the left and a regiment at the head of the other column would swing to the right, clearing the Confederates from their lines on either side of the flattened fort. Then the rest of the division would drive to the top of Cemetery Hill, with Burnside's three other divisions following.

Although no final decision had been made about the attack, on Wednesday afternoon,

July 27, Pleasants received orders to begin loading the tunnel with four tons of gunpowder. It took his men six hours, until 10 p.m., to place the 320 kegs of black powder. The kegs were concentrated in eight magazines, each containing 1,000 pounds of powder. Four magazines were placed in each of two lateral galleries that extended almost 40 feet north and south from the end of the main tunnel. The magazines would be detonated by gunpowder-filled wooden troughs leading from the main gallery, where a 98-foot fuse ran toward the mine entrance. Instead of high-quality, continuous blasting fuse, Pleasants was given 10-foot lengths of low-grade fuse, which his men had to splice.

To prevent the force of the explosion from being vented harmlessly out the mouth of the

Deep trenches, like this one opposite Elliott's Salient, helped conceal the miners from enemy view as they moved to and from the tunnel. The dugout at center, replete with a brick chimney, was one of the more elaborate shelters that shielded troops on line from the elements. "At sultry midday or during a rainfall," a soldier said, "one might look up or down the trenches without seeing anybody but the sentinel."

mine, earth was tamped into the ends of the side galleries and the last 34 feet of the main gallery. This work went on all night, and it was not finished until Thursday evening.

On Friday, July 29, Meade issued orders implementing Burnside's plan for the explosion of the mine and an attack. It was to take place at dawn the next day. First, however, there would be a great deal of preliminary maneuvering. Major General Gouverneur K. Warren, holding the Federal left, was to concentrate as much of his V Corps as possible on his right, near Burnside's corps; Hancock, returning with II Corps from north of the James, was to take Major General Edward O. C. Ord's place on the right so that Ord's XVIII Corps, reinforced by one division of X Corps, could support Burnside;

and Sheridan was to take the Cavalry Corps all the way around Petersburg and make a secondary assault from the southwest. Federal cannon were concentrated at the main point of attack under the army's chief of artillery, Brigadier General Henry J. Hunt.

Meade told Burnside to "spring his mine" at 3:30 a.m. Immediately thereafter he was to "move rapidly upon the breach, seize the crest in the rear and effect a lodgement there." Warren would support Burnside on the left, Ord on the right. Meade also promised to get engineers from headquarters, since an assault across ground that had been the scene of trench warfare for a month was going to need their help.

Thus far, although the unfriendly relationship between Burnside and Meade, who had once been his subordinate, remained prickly at best, things were going well. But then, with less than 24 hours until jump-off, Burnside was enraged to learn that Meade had made changes in his plan. Meade insisted that Burnside replace the division that he had chosen to lead the attack.

This was a complicated issue. Several days earlier, Burnside had selected his freshest division, commanded by Brigadier General Edward Ferrero, to spearhead the advance. Burnside had explained that his three other divisions had been in the trenches and under fire for 36 days, during which time an average of 30 men had been killed or wounded every day. By contrast, Ferrero's two brigades had been in the rear and had been able to rehearse their crucial role.

The problem, as Meade saw it, was twofold. Ferrero's men were not only fresh, they were completely inexperienced, having never been in battle. An assault on which so much depended, said Meade, should be led by the most seasoned troops available.

Even more significant, in Meade's view, was that Ferrero's men were black — he led the only division of U.S. Colored Troops in the Army of the Potomac. It might be said, Meade fretted, "that we were shoving these people ahead to get killed because we did not care anything about them."

When Burnside insisted vehemently on his original plan, Meade consented to take the matter up with Grant. Hearing nothing, Burnside assumed by the next day that the matter had been dismissed, and he proceeded with his preparations. But at midmorning Friday, Meade dropped a double bombshell on his corps commander. Not only had Grant agreed that the black troops should not lead the attack but Meade also

ordered that there be no lateral movements to clear the enemy trenches. Instead, the whole force should drive straight ahead to the crest of Cemetery Hill.

Burnside was devastated. He had always excelled at making plans on paper, and this had been a good one; but he had never functioned well when forced to improvise, and Meade's changes unraveled him completely.

Unwilling to choose among his three other division commanders — Brigadier Generals Robert Potter, James Ledlie and Orlando Willcox — Burnside ducked the momentous responsibility by having them draw straws. The man thus selected to lead the assault was Ledlie, perhaps the least competent division commander in the Army of the Potomac, a known weakling, drinker and coward.

Burnside knew Ledlie's reputation but gave him the critical assignment anyway. Far worse, he did nothing to prepare his troops for moving across the tangle of fortifications. Ignoring Meade's specific orders, Burnside did not see to the opening of his parapets and abatis for the attackers to pass through. The promised engineers from headquarters never materialized, and Burnside failed to order his own engineers to accompany the assault and help with the opening of the enemy works. He did not even distribute entrenching tools for use on the bare hilltop that was the objective. He simply told Ledlie to lead the way, with Potter following and bearing to the right, and Willcox next, bearing to the left. The rest was left to the division commanders — and to chance.

On the afternoon of the 29th Meade went to Burnside's headquarters to impress upon him and his senior commanders that, as Meade put it later, the operation "was one purely of time." They must gain the crest of

Major General Bushrod Johnson, whose division defended the section of the Confederate line targeted by the Federal mining operation, seemed strangely detached from the problems confronting his command. "He was barely known by sight to his men," one Virginian remarked.

Brigadier General Stephen Elliott Jr., one of Bushrod Johnson's subordinates, held the vulnerable salient that bore his name. Elliott was no stranger to tight spots: Before his transfer to Petersburg from Charleston, he had led the besieged Confederate forces at Fort Sumter for eight months.

Cemetery Hill quickly, before the enemy could recover from the confusion caused by the explosion. Failing that, Meade said, they must get back to their lines quickly; above all, they must not simply try to hold on to the shattered section of the enemy's line. As events would show, none of Meade's imperatives had any effect on Burnside.

After a tense, wakeful night, Colonel Pleasants entered the tunnel at 3:15 a.m. on Saturday, lit the fuse and came running out. It should have taken 15 minutes for the 98 feet of fuse to burn, but at 3:30 nothing happened. Another 15 minutes passed and still nothing. It was impossible to know whether the fuse had gone out or was burning at a slower rate than expected. "Pleasants became like a maniac," recalled a soldier in the 48th Pennsylvania. At 4:15 he allowed two volunteers to go into the tunnel to investigate. The fuse had gone out at a splice. They relit it and sprinted for safety.

At 4:40 a.m., someone on the Federal line yelled, "There she goes!" and another soldier reported feeling a "jar like an earthquake." A Union staff officer, Major Oliver C. Bosbyshell, wrote that "a vast cloud of earth is borne upward, one hundred feet in the air, presenting the appearance of an outspread umbrella, descending in the twinkling of an eye with a heavy thud! Then, from hundreds of cannons' mouths, with a deafening roar, the iron hail poured into the rebel lines."

The explosion obliterated the tip of Elliott's Salient, which housed Pegram's four-gun battery, and paralyzed half of Elliott's brigade of infantry. At least 22 gunners of Pegram's Battery, along with 256 men of the 18th and the 22nd South Carolina — the regiments flanking the guns — died in the blast. Scores of others were injured, many having been lofted into the air to fall to earth again with tons of dirt and debris.

Colonel Fitz William McMaster of the 17th South Carolina, next in line to the 18th, recalled the men's "utmost consternation" after the explosion. "Some scampered out of the lines; some, paralyzed with fear, vaguely scratched at the counterscarp as if trying to escape. Smoke and dust filled the air."

The way into Petersburg lay open to Burnside and IX Corps. But the blast had disconcerted them almost as badly as it had the Confederates. According to Lieutenant William H. Powell, one of Ledlie's aides, the cloud raised by the explosion "appeared as if it would descend immediately upon the troops waiting to make the charge."

Some of Ledlie's men broke and ran to the rear. The others were too stunned to move. It took 10 minutes, perhaps more, before they were able to re-form and advance.

Then the attackers paid the price for their commanders' failure to open the fortifications. Hasty steps had to be fashioned with muskets so that the men could climb out of their own trenches. This effort destroyed their formations, and the men, already deployed by the flank and forced to move forward in long columns, dashed forward in ragged spurts, two or three at a time. They raced the hundred yards across the open incline, clambered atop a 12-foot-high wall of dirt thrown up by the explosion, looked over — and were transfixed.

Where Pegram's redan had been, there yawned an enormous hole, 200 feet long, 50 feet wide and 25 to 30 feet deep in the center: the Crater. It was filled, Lieutenant Powell wrote, "with dust, great blocks of clay,

The eruption of the mine under the Confederate defenses at daybreak on July 30 raises a plume of debris on the horizon as Union officers look on in the foreground. The explosion signaled a devastating barrage by Federal batteries, including the 10-inch mortars at center, emplaced between traverses built of wicker gabions.

guns, broken carriages, projecting timbers, and men buried in various ways — some up to their necks, others to their waists, and some with only their feet and legs protruding from the earth." Most of the entombed were dead, but some were emerging from their shock and struggling to break free.

What little sense of purpose and organization the Federals had possessed as they straggled forward now evaporated. The men of Ledlie's lead brigade stood on the rim of the Crater, gawking. This forced the regiments behind them to mill around in confusion until the brigade commander, Colonel Elisha G. Marshall, roared at them to make their way down into the Crater. Here too, the men simply milled about, extricating wounded Confederates and hunting souvenirs.

A portion of Colonel Marshall's brigade clambered up the far side of the Crater and began to form up for a further advance. Beyond the Crater the Federals saw what one of them described as "a perfect honeycomb of bomb proofs, trenches, covered ways, sleeping holes and little alleys running in every direction," all partially filled with debris from the explosion. Behind the honeycomb, forming a rear wall to the area of devastation, stood the newly built cavalier and retrenchment. With much difficulty, Colonel Marshall got his men into rough battle lines and pushed into the trenches and covered ways. The 14th New York Heavy Artillery found that one of the fort's cannon and its magazine, though partly buried, remained serviceable. The Federals dug out the gun and, under the direction of Sergeant Wesley Stanley of Company D, began to fire at the Confederates visible in the rear. To the right of the Crater, Lieutenant Colonel Gilbert P. Robinson of the 3rd Maryland Battalion

pushed his way into the Confederate trench with parties of skirmishers. The Marylanders, armed with Spencer rifles, were able to force their way 300 yards forward, leapfrogging from traverse to traverse.

But by this time, the Confederates in the trenches on either side of the Crater had recovered. The dusty survivors of the 22nd South Carolina, directed by their only remaining officer, Captain James N. Shedd, threw up a barricade of sandbags across the main trench south of the breach. To the north, the 17th South Carolina spread out into the connecting trenches and traverses, hoping to confine the attackers to the Crater.

At this point the Federal cause sorely needed a measure of leadership, but it was not to come from General Ledlie. He was huddled in a bombproof far to the rear, comforting himself with a bottle of rum. He sat there in safety while his division fell into confusion and the divisions of Potter and Willcox trickled forward past him.

Federal artillerists had opened fire with 160 guns immediately after the mine exploded, to keep the enemy's guns from firing effectively at the advancing infantry. Nevertheless, two Confederate batteries — Davidson's, 400 yards south of the Crater, and Wright's, about 500 yards to the north — unleashed a vicious crossfire on the slope between the Crater and the Federal lines. Confederate Major David N. Walker, commanding Davidson's Battery, wrote later that his gunners, along with those of Captain S. T. Wright, "were sweeping the open field like a tornado." Soon, Walker wrote, the field "looked like an inclined plane of dead men."

From a hillside 300 yards south of the Crater, Colonel John T. Goode formed the

The resilient Brigadier General William Bartlett, captured after his cork leg was crushed by shellfire, was helped from the Crater by a Confederate who thought him freshly wounded. "I could see no evidence of pain in his face," the man wrote, "and remarked to him that he must have nerves of steel." Bartlett confessed that he had suffered the real injury two years earlier, at Yorktown.

59th Virginia in a ditch running perpendicular to the Confederate trench. From there it could open an enfilading fire on any Federals attempting to form in the open ground behind the Crater. Nearby, a single gun commanded by Captain Samuel D. Preston of the 34th Virginia opened with canister from the front-line trench into the flank of Federal troops advancing toward the Crater.

General Potter's division had tried to bear to the right of Ledlie's advance across the deadly field, but it had encountered resistance from Elliott's surviving South Carolinians. The attacking soldiers plunged into the confusing maze of covered ways, rifle pits and trenches. Disoriented, intermixed with the enemy and fighting hand to hand, they got no farther. As Lieutenant Powell recalled, "There were so many angles and traverses there that in one there were Union troops while in the next there were Confederates. I saw myself the muskets of both sides almost crossed at the angles, while the men were obscured from each other." General Willcox's division was similarly stalled on

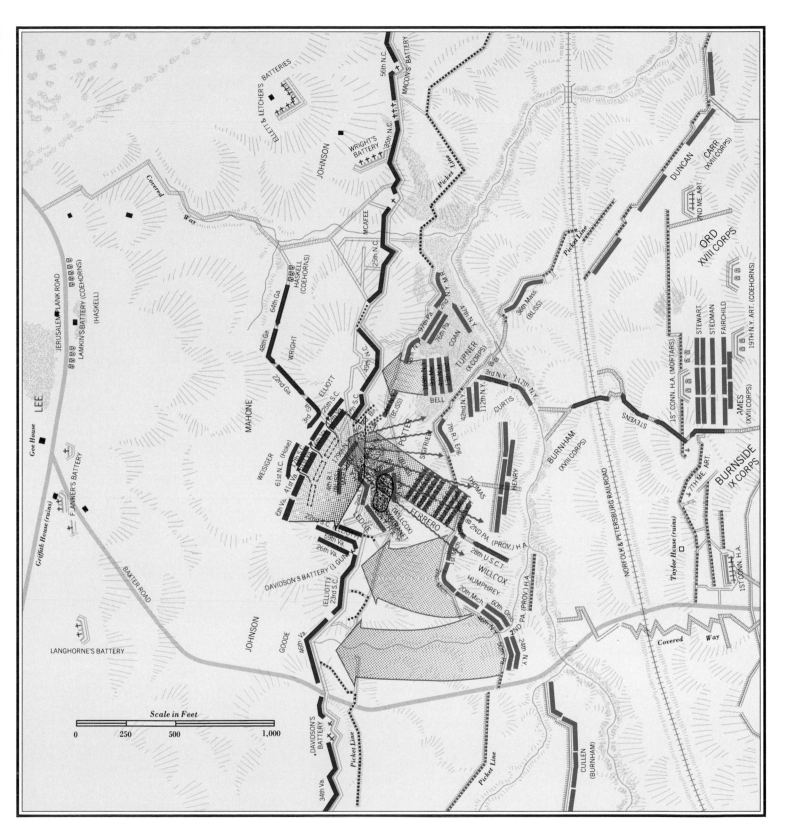

The fighting at the Crater reached a critical juncture about 9 a.m., as Ferrero's black division moved up to join the battle. By now the Confederates had shored up their line on either side of the Crater and were fending off the Federal thrusts. Simultaneously, Confederate General Mahone was launching a counterattack: Weisiger's Virginia brigade collided with the front line of Ferrero's advancing troops west of the Crater and drove them back, dashing any remaining Union hopes for a breakthrough.

the left of the Crater, unable to advance beyond its own lines.

About 7 a.m., Brigadier General John W. Turner, whose X Corps division had been temporarily assigned to Ord's XVIII Corps, reached the front. He was blocked by a mass of soldiers and dashed to the Crater to reconnoiter. He wrote later that inside the cavity "every point that could give cover to a man was occupied. There was no movement toward Cemetery Hill: The troops were all in confusion and lying down."

Turner saw Ferrero's black infantry appear at the lip of the Crater. Ferrero was absent; he had stopped to keep General

Ledlie company in the bombproof. The black troops, Turner recalled, "literally came falling over into this crater on their hands and knees; they were so thick in there that a man could not walk." Disgusted by the turmoil, Turner went back to the main Federal lines and learned that General Meade had ordered both Ord and Warren to attack, on either side of IX Corps. Accordingly, Turner pushed his brigades toward the right of the Crater.

Three hours had passed since the explosion of the mine, and the Federals had only succeeded in cramming an estimated 10,000 troops into the area of the Crater. Mean-

Federal Generals James Ledlie (*left*) and Edward Ferrero were censured by a court of inquiry after the Battle of the Crater for hiding in a bombproof during the attack. A surgeon who was with them that morning testified that they had asked him for "stimulants" and he had given them rum. Ledlie soon took sick leave, a move one officer in his division called a "heavy loss to the enemy."

80

LOOK HERE, AND HERE.

GEN. VAN SKULKO, OF THE POTOMAC ARMY, AT THE BATTLE OF JULY 30.

Where Gen. Grant intended him to be— AND *Where he really was, all the time.*

while, the Confederates were on the verge of mounting a counterattack.

General Elliott had survived the explosion, but he fell wounded after ordering the 26th and the 17th South Carolina to leave the trenches north of the Crater and defend the open ground to the rear. Colonel McMaster took over Elliott's brigade and organized a fragile line across the throat of the blasted salient in the retrenchment 200 yards to the rear. McMaster posted a second, even thinner line in a ravine 100 yards to the west. For three hours, these few hundred scattered troops were all that lay between the Army of the Potomac and the streets of Petersburg.

General Lee had rushed to the field at 6 a.m. and had ordered General William Mahone, whose division held the Confederate right, to send two of his brigades north to reinforce Bushrod Johnson's threatened division at the Crater. Mahone responded immediately, saying, "I can't send my brigades to General Johnson—I will go with them myself." On reaching Johnson's headquarters on the Jerusalem Plank Road, however, Mahone was shocked to see the commander of the breached line sitting down to breakfast, evincing little interest in what was going on at the front. When Mahone asked to be shown the way to the Crater, Johnson detailed a lieutenant to guide Mahone and returned to his breakfast.

Peppered by Federal shot and shell from the continuing bombardment, Mahone took his brigades north along the Jerusalem Plank Road to a covered way that led to the left toward the location of Wright's Battery. Halfway there they turned southeast, filing into the ravine held by McMaster's reserves. There Brigadier General Davis A. Weisiger's Virginia brigade of Mahone's division formed a line of battle and Brigadier General Ambrose R. Wright's Georgians started to file in behind them to take position on their right. It was approximately 8:30 a.m.

The Virginians faced a daunting sight. Behind the lip of the Crater, "the battle flags seemed almost as thick as cornstalks in a row," recalled Private Richard B. Davis, a sharpshooter with the 12th Virginia. "The whole face of the earth, including the ditch which our men formerly occupied, fairly teemed with the enemy." Mahone ordered his men to fix bayonets, to prepare to charge and to hold their fire until they reached the enemy line 200 yards away.

Meanwhile, in the Crater, the brigade commanders of the black troops, Colonels Henry G. Thomas and Joshua K. Sigfried, received new orders from General Ferrero's hideout in the rear. Advance, said Ferrero grandly, and take the crest of Cemetery Hill.

Struggling mightily to push his troops through the sea of stalled men — three entire divisions of them — Colonel Thomas managed to get two of his regiments and part of a third, perhaps 200 men in all, formed up beyond the Crater, and ordered them to charge. Remarkably, they did.

Wright's Georgia brigade was not yet in line of battle when Weisiger's Virginians

heard the shout and saw the Federal charge begin. But the Confederates knew immediately that if they did not halt this movement in its tracks, the momentum of the Federal column would sweep them away.

"The men sprang to their feet and cried, 'Charge, boys!' and away we went over the field," recalled Private Davis. "I shall never forget the magnificent appearance of that long line of tattered uniforms as it swept in splendid form across the field in the face of a tremendous fire that with every step was thinning our ranks."

The Confederate infantry was not yet fir-

Major General William Mahone *(left)*, the pugnacious son of a tavern-keeper, lived up to his reputation by rushing to the Crater with the Virginia brigade of Davis Weisiger *(above)* and the Georgia brigade of Ambrose Wright *(below)*. "Whenever Mahone moves out," an admirer remarked, "someone is apt to be hurt."

ing, but the moment the black troops came over the parapet they were in the sights of a battery deployed along the Jerusalem Plank Road 500 yards to the west. These guns staggered the attacking troops, although a Southern observer reported later that "a single private, with his musket at support arms, made the charge, running all the way to the guns and jumping into the sunken road between them, where he was felled with a rammer staff."

The two infantry charges collided in the warren of Confederate rifle pits and trenches west and north of the Crater. The attacking Federals were heavily outnumbered outside the Crater, and they received no reinforcements from within it. One officer who was trying to get the men cowering at the bottom of the Crater to move forward wrote later, "You might as well have tried to get bees out of a hive and form them into line."

Isolated and hit hard, the black regiments lost heart, broke and ran. Mahone's Confederates were close behind them. Major William H. Etheredge, commanding the 41st Virginia, jumped into the trench with the first sergeant of Company D. They landed in a crowd of Federal soldiers. "The Yanks were as thick as they could stand," recalled Etheredge, and the sergeant was instantly shot. "Just then the man that killed the Sergeant stooped down and picked up a musket, evidently with the intention of killing me." In desperation Etheredge grabbed two Federals who stood frozen near him, "and kept them so close together it was impossible for him to kill me without endangering the lives of his own men. Just at that moment our men were jumping into the ditch like frogs. One of them jumped just behind me, and I sang out to him at the top of my voice to kill

the man in front of me." The man fired, saving Etheredge.

The Confederates were startled, then enraged, to discover that they were fighting black troops. "I saw Confederates beating and shooting at the negro soldiers as the latter, terror-stricken, rushed away from them," wrote Private George S. Bernard of the 12th Virginia. Many of the Confederates would not accept surrender from a black: Bernard saw an unarmed man pleading for his life while one Confederate beat him with a ramrod and another deliberately reloaded his musket and shot the distraught Federal in the stomach.

The Confederate charge had struck just as General Turner was leading his division forward on Burnside's right. The precipitous flight of the black troops broke the line of IX Corps soldiers in the ditch north of the Crater, and they in turn touched off a stampede by two of Turner's brigades, which fled back to the main Union line.

The Federals near the crest of the Crater "were loading and firing as fast as they could," remembered Lieutenant Freeman S. Bowley, a white officer of the 30th U.S. Colored Troops. "The men were dropping thick and fast, most of them shot through the head. Every man that was shot rolled down the steep sides to the bottom, and in places they were piled up three and four deep. The cries of the wounded, pressed down under the dead, were piteous in the extreme."

One of General Potter's officers, Colonel George W. Field of the 4th Rhode Island Volunteers, had held a position about 100 yards behind the Crater. Mahone's attack forced his command back, and Field tried to get his men to rescue several of the regiment's wounded. "Who will follow

Advancing around their flag with its severed staff, Confederates of the 12th Virginia clash at the edge of the Crater with the Federal vanguard, including the black troops of Ferrero's division. The 12th Virginia's broken flagstaff was spliced with a ramrod (*above*) during the ensuing action and planted on earthworks the regiment had reclaimed. Color Sergeant William Smith examined the flag that night and counted 75 bullet holes in the fabric, which was subsequently mended.

me?'' he shouted. One of Field's soldiers, Corporal George H. Allen, recalled that "with sword uplifted, he advanced one step and fell dead."

The Confederates continued to roll forward. From the Crater's south end, a covered way extended west to the retrenchment 200 yards away, and now the Virginians were driving up this traverse to within 20 yards of the Crater itself. Ordered to build a breastwork across the mouth of the traverse, the Federals, according to Bowley, began "by throwing up lumps of clay, but it was slow work. Someone called out, 'Put in the dead men,' and a large number of dead, white and black, Union and rebel, were piled into the trench. This made a partial shelter," he concluded, from which the Federals stopped the Confederate advance.

For nearly five hours General Meade, back at Burnside's headquarters with General Grant, had been trying frantically to get from Burnside — who was at a forward command post with a 14-gun battery on his main line — some indication of what was happening. Meade had ordered a telegraph line strung between the two locations, but despite this capacity for instant communication he could not get Burnside to give him any news. "What is the delay in your column moving?" Meade had asked at 6:50 a.m.;

COLONEL JOHN HASKELL

Lethal Work of a Mobile Mortar

Shortly after 10 a.m. on July 30, as General William Mahone was preparing to renew the Confederate counterattack against Union troops in the Crater, a young artillery officer named John Haskell offered his services to Mahone. Colonel Haskell had lost his right arm at Gaines's Mill in 1862, but he had lost none of his fighting spirit; Mahone considered him a brilliant soldier, "always hunting a place where he could strike a blow at our adversary." Now such an opportunity was at hand: Mahone suggested that Haskell move two of his compact Coehorn mortars to within 20 yards of the Crater, where they could shell the Federals with deadly accuracy.

The Coehorn was the perfect weapon for this arduous task. It weighed only 300 pounds and was fitted with handles that enabled four men to carry it to points in the trenchworks that could not be reached by gun carriages. It could loft an 18-pound shell over a parapet and was brutally effective at short range.

Haskell and his men moved their mortars ever nearer the Crater, stopping to fire and reducing the powder charge after every advance. Eventually the shells rose so sluggishly, Haskell wrote, that it seemed "they could not get to the enemy." Yet they did, raising cries that were plainly audible to the gunners. Not until the lethal little mortars had taken a steep toll did Mahone commit his full force to the successful attack.

and 40 minutes later he had demanded, "What is the obstacle?"

When Burnside did respond he dissembled: "The main body of General Potter's division is beyond the Crater." He evaded the issue of speed: "I am fully alive to the importance of it." And he took umbrage: "The latter remark of your note was unofficerlike and ungentlemanly." Not until 9 a.m. did Burnside transmit any definite information, and then it was stunning: "Many of the Ninth and Eighteenth Corps are retiring before the enemy."

Meade was appalled. "That was the first information I had received," he said later, "that there had been any collision with the enemy, or that there was any enemy present." At 9:30 he told Generals Burnside and Ord that they ought to retreat, "taking every precaution to get the men back safely." At 9:45 he made the order to Burnside peremptory: "Withdraw to your own intrenchments." Meade left it to Burnside to pick the time, but for 11 hours he would not get an acknowledgment, a reply or any further information from the IX Corps commander.

At 10 a.m., Mahone unleashed Wright's Georgia brigade. It was supposed to charge the 50 yards of captured Confederate entrenchments south of the Crater, on the right of the Virginia brigade. The advance ran into such withering fire, however, that the Georgians were deflected to their left and came in behind the Virginians.

But the Federals in the Crater were losing the will to continue the fight. The day had become unbearably hot, and the canteens were empty; the Confederates now opened with additional mortars, which had been brought up to extremely close range. A few Federals tried to run back to their lines, just 100 yards away. "But, to leave," wrote Lieutenant Bowley, "they had to run up a slope in full view of the enemy that now surrounded us on three sides; nearly every man who attempted it fell back riddled with bullets." The same fate befell those who tried to bring water or ammunition into the Crater.

With two brigades, General Mahone had immobilized three Federal corps. Burnside's IX Corps was cowering leaderless in and around the Crater; on its right, Ord's XVIII Corps had been driven back to the main Federal lines; and on its left, Warren's V Corps had never been able to mount an attack. The cannonading continued, but the musketry now became desultory. The opposing lines,

24-POUNDER COEHORN MORTAR MODEL 1838

in many places huddled on either side of the same embankment, took to spearing each other by lofting muskets with fixed bayonets over the crest. It seemed to Colonel McMaster, "the laziest fight I ever saw; we longed for hand grenades."

Now Brigadier General John C. C. Sanders' Alabama brigade came up to Mahone's position in the ravine, and at 1 p.m. Mahone ordered it to charge the Crater. Sanders' men were joined by the 61st North Carolina, dispatched from General Robert Hoke's division. Elliott's beleaguered 17th South Carolina joined in as well. By that time Burnside had at last responded to Meade's withdrawal order — by telling the hapless brigade com-

manders in the Crater to get out as best they could. They were trying to figure out how to do this when the fresh Confederates poured over the rim of the Crater.

Some of the Federals had no choice but to fight hand to hand; others tried to surrender, while several hundred simply ran for their lives. "The slaughter was fearful," recalled one of Mahone's officers, especially among unarmed and unresisting blacks. In some places the dead were said to be piled eight deep before the remaining Federals surrendered. By 2 o'clock or shortly thereafter the battle was over.

General Lee reported crisply to Richmond: "We have retaken the salient and

At left, half-buried corpses and severed limbs litter the Crater after the battle. Among the Federal units trapped there by enemy fire was Company I of the 57th Massachusetts (*inset*); it had already been reduced to a handful of troops after beginning the campaign with 86 men in early May. The entire regiment numbered only 100 or so when it charged the Crater, and within hours half of that force was lost, caught in what one survivor described as "a seething cauldron of struggling, dying men."

driven the enemy back to his lines with loss." Every man in the fight, Lee said, "made himself a hero." Within hours, the Confederates were entrenching a new line — in front of the Crater.

"It was the saddest affair I have witnessed in the War," Grant wired to Halleck the next day. He counted 3,500 men killed, wounded or missing, compared with Confederate losses of about 1,500, and he had no gains to show for it. The attack had been a fumble from the beginning, and though Grant had done little to assure success of the plan, he demanded an immediate court of inquiry.

The court laid the blame on General Burn-side, for failing to form a proper line of battle, for neglecting to open a path through the Federal obstacles, for not using engineers to negotiate the enemy entrenchments and for disobeying several of Meade's orders. Once again, Burnside was relieved of command — for the last time in the War. The court also censured Generals Ledlie and Ferrero for hiding out in their bombproof and General Willcox for lack of leadership.

Grant believed that the failure to take Petersburg, and perhaps end the War, was inexcusable. "Such opportunity for carrying fortifications I have never seen," he told Halleck, "and do not expect again to have."

Vestiges of a Volcanic Upheaval

The brutal nature of the Battle of the Crater is recorded not only in the accounts of the soldiers who survived but also in the artifacts collected from the site. A selection of these homely articles of war is displayed here and on the following pages, set against a backdrop of contemporary engravings of the mine's explosion and the fighting that followed.

The objects on these two pages tell of the grueling labor that led to the debacle. Wielding their picks by the light of candles in the cramped tunnel, Federal miners filled countless crates with soil, while above them both sides went about the dull business of entrenching in preparation for the fight that was to come. At intervals the tedium was broken, as hungry men fried up some hardtack with a bit of fat in their pans or slyly poked their shovels above the lip of the trench to draw a burst of enemy fire.

The culmination of all this activity was a day of carnage, its devastation documented by the battered relics shown on the next two pages. Some of these articles were found among the remains of Federal casualties who were buried in a shallow common grave within the Crater.

CRATE FOUND IN TUNNEL

BOTTLES USED BY MINERS
AS CANDLEHOLDERS

FRYING PAN WITH FOLDING
HANDLE FOUND IN CRATER

ENTRENCHING SHOVEL

MINING PICK

91

ENFIELD RIFLE

FEDERAL CANTEEN

INITIALED CAP POUCH

BELT FRAGMENT WITH U.S. PLATE

92

FEDERAL CARTRIDGE BOX

CONFEDERATE SOLDIER'S SHOE

93

Tightening the Noose

"If Hancock's heart could have been examined there would have been written on it 'REAMS,' as plainly as the deep scars received at Gettysburg and other fields were visible."

MAJOR GENERAL HENRY HETH, C.S.A., ON THE BATTLE OF REAMS'S STATION

Something seemed terribly wrong with the Army of the Potomac. As Captain George K. Leet of Grant's staff put it a few days after the Crater fiasco, "There were screws loose somewhere and the machine would not work." The most visible problem was the army's extreme weariness after three months of savage campaigning; the constant work and alarms of trench warfare made rest and recuperation impossible. Attrition from casualties and expired enlistments continued, and by early August the Army of the Potomac's effective strength had been reduced to fewer than 40,000 men. Moreover, the replacements were of the worst imaginable quality: sullen draftees, paid substitutes and bounty jumpers — all with little training and less motivation.

The enervation of the army was made worse by a pervasive rancor that infected its second-echelon leaders. The provost marshal general, Brigadier General Marsena Patrick, lamented the jealousy of the corps commanders "against each other and against Meade." Patrick, ever the pessimist, had accurately predicted the failure of the mine attack on July 30. "The bad blood that exists between Meade and Burnside," he had warned, would prevent "unanimity of counsels or concert of action."

Officers still loyal to Major General George B. McClellan, the army's deposed commander, disliked the newly arrived Grant men; the Westerners in turn derided the Easterners, and everyone seemed to disparage Meade, spreading rumors that he was about to be relieved or transferred. Nor was Grant immune. One general accused him — again — of getting drunk; another compared his detached style of leadership to that of Nero fiddling while Rome burned.

As sulfurous as were the Union army's rivalries, the national politics with which they were entwined were worse. With the presidential election three months away, the army was split by the continuing devotion of some to the likely Democratic candidate, General McClellan, and the loyalty of others to the incumbent Commander in Chief, Abraham Lincoln.

Lincoln supporters were especially dismayed by the failure of the army to achieve a clear victory in the spring campaign and by its inability to protect Washington from Jubal Early's raid or to punish Early for his audacity. On the day of the disaster at the Crater, Early's cavalry had ridden boldly into Pennsylvania and burned the town of Chambersburg.

The pressure on Grant was enormous. Yet every time he tried to rid himself of an incompetent general, such as Benjamin Butler, or to reorganize the commands around Washington, whose inefficiency had paralyzed the pursuit of Early, he was stymied by equally strong pressures to avoid offending important political constituencies.

Grant appeared unaffected by either the reverses in the field or the rivalries in camp. "We will peg away, and end this matter," he

This fragment from a Confederate shell, shown full-scale, struck Lieutenant Colonel Richard Thompson, of the 12th New Jersey, in the stomach during the battle at Reams's Station. Thompson recovered from the painful wound and returned to limited duty before the siege ended.

wrote to a boyhood friend. "Everything looks favorable." Grant simply ignored most of the squabbling among his corps commanders and staff officers. But with the same quiet relentlessness he showed in battle, he bore down on those problems that interfered with his destruction of the enemy.

Thus, during the first week of August, Grant rammed home a solution for the problems that Early was posing. He ordered the four military departments merged into one and dispatched his energetic Cavalry Corps commander, Major General Philip H. Sheridan, to take charge.

There was little use for cavalrymen in trench warfare and a great need for them in running Early to ground; therefore, Sheridan took with him two of the army's three divisions of troopers. His orders from Grant were to follow Early to the death, then lay waste to the Shenandoah Valley. With the Army of the Shenandoah augmented by VI Corps, XIX Corps and the two cavalry divisions, Sheridan went after Early with almost 40,000 men.

Robert E. Lee could not afford to lose either his Shenandoah granary or Early's corps. Despite the fact that Confederate manpower on the Richmond-Petersburg line was already stretched impossibly thin, Lee found a way to help Early. He sent Major General J. B. Kershaw's division of infantry from Anderson's corps and Fitzhugh Lee's cavalry division to Culpeper, where they would be in position to move to the Valley or return to Richmond, wherever the danger was greater. Lee knew his opponent by now; he did not doubt for a moment that trouble was coming, and soon.

It came on August 14, largely because of Grant's mistaken assessment of what Lee had done. Grant was informed that Lieutenant General Richard Anderson's entire corps had been sent to the Shenandoah, and he concluded that the Confederate line north of the James River must be held by no more than 8,500 men. Concerned about Sheridan's safety and determined to keep up his alternate jabbing of Lee — now south, now north, of the James — Grant ordered Meade to unleash General Hancock north of the river once again.

Grant's immediate objective was to force Lee to recall the forces he had sent north and to prevent the dispatching of any more. But Grant also hoped Hancock would reach Richmond this time, and he ordered Meade to attack Petersburg if Hancock's actions brought about "almost the entire abandonment" of the town.

Eight miles south of Richmond, at the first bend in the James, the main Confederate line of fortifications straddled the river, anchored on Chaffin's Bluff to the north and Drewry's Bluff to the south. Hancock's objective was the supposedly weakened line extending northeast from Chaffin's Bluff.

Four miles downriver, to the east, a pontoon bridge now linked Butler's Federal forces on Bermuda Hundred with the part of his X Corps posted north of the river at Deep Bottom. In preparation for the offensive, Major General David Birney took the rest of X Corps, along with Hancock's artillery and Brigadier General David M. Gregg's cavalry division, across the bridge from Bermuda Hundred on the night of August 13.

Meanwhile, Hancock's II Corps conducted an elaborate ruse to make the Confederates believe the men were being sent north to reinforce Sheridan. Indeed, that is what the

95

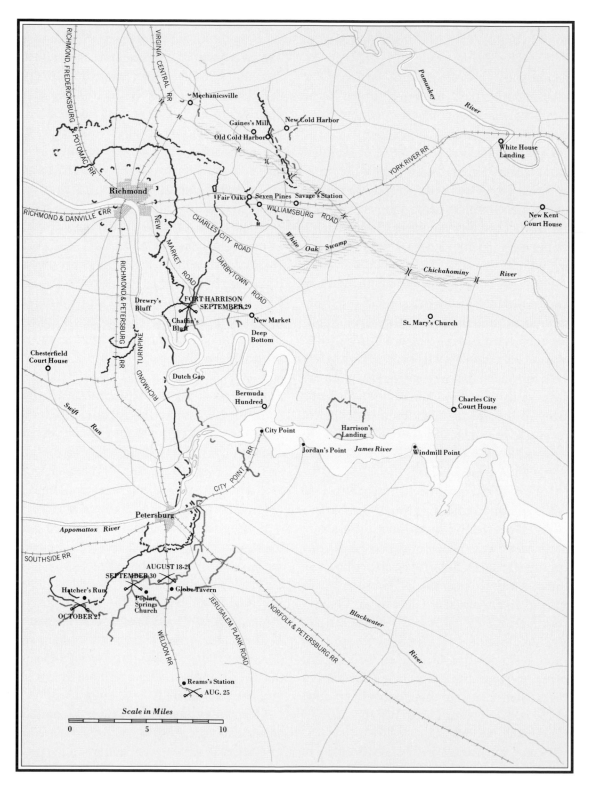

In late summer of 1864 General Lee's forces were stretched to the breaking point in layers of defensive lines that extended from Richmond to Petersburg. The Federals hammered at Lee with coordinated attacks, both north of the James, at Fort Harrison, and south of the river, at the Weldon Railroad and Hatcher's Run. By November, Grant's repeated blows had softened the Confederate defenses, but they failed to achieve the breakthrough he sought.

Federal troops thought as they marched through the lingering heat and the pervasive dust to the wharves at City Point, a half-dozen miles northeast of their Petersburg lines. There they filed aboard steam transports that took them downstream, toward the Chesapeake Bay.

Soon, however, the steamers hove to in midstream and waited. After a time, a tugboat brought new orders; the transports came about and headed upstream, and the men understood where they were really going. They were to land at Deep Bottom and move out from there at dawn on August 14. Low water caused difficulties in the disembarkation, however, and it was 9 a.m. before the men were on shore and formed up.

The Federal order of battle had Birney with X Corps on the left, closest to the James. Brigadier General Gershom Mott, commanding Hancock's 3rd Division, was in the center, with orders to push forward on the New Market road toward Richmond. And Brigadier General Francis Barlow, who in General John Gibbon's temporary absence was leading the 1st and 2nd Divisions of II Corps, held the right. While Gregg's cavalry covered the extreme right and looked for a chance to make a dash toward Richmond, Barlow was to attack the enemy at Fussell's Mill on the Darbytown road, which paralleled the New Market road a mile and a half to the north.

General Barlow, a Harvard-educated lawyer who had enlisted as a private in 1861, was one of the best officers in the Northern army. But he had suffered more than most in this war. He had been severely wounded in 1862 at Antietam and in 1863 at Gettysburg, where he was left on the field for dead. Confederate General John B. Gordon had found

him there, tended to him and arranged to get him into the care of Mrs. Barlow, who was a nurse traveling with the Federal Army. It had taken Barlow more than six months, with his wife constantly at his side, to recover. Then in July of 1864 his fragile health was shaken again by the news that his wife had contracted typhoid fever and had died.

Barlow's attack at Fussell's Mill was to be the key to Hancock's offensive. With all the delays, it was midday on August 14 before the advancing Federals made contact with the enemy; and when they did, it was clear at once that there were more Confederates present than the Federals expected. Birney and Mott, on the left and center, ran into a full Confederate division commanded by Major General C. W. Field. Another division, under Major General Cadmus Marcellus Wilcox, was at Chaffin's Bluff, and still more troops were coming. Birney and Mott could make no headway, and when Barlow finally got his assault started on the right, he fumbled it.

Barlow had been instructed to attack in force along the Darbytown road. Instead, he had formed a line of battle that extended from Mott's right flank to the road. In the thick woods Barlow's men, many of them indifferent recruits led by inexperienced officers, became confused and hopelessly strung out. Barlow had 10,000 men in his two divisions; but after forming his line, he had only a single brigade left with which to attack at Fussell's Mill.

Two regiments of Confederate cavalry were at the mill, and the Federals quickly drove them away. There was little time to enjoy the victory, however. Field pulled a brigade out of the right of his line and sent it swinging north, where it charged into the

flank of one of Barlow's brigades and chased it back. The move had weakened the Confederate line in front of Birney's men; they doubled their efforts and were able to take some Confederate entrenchments and four guns, but they could go no farther.

Although the Federal attack was stalled, it was having the desired effect on Lee. He concluded, after exchanging a flurry of telegraph messages with Field, that this new threat to Richmond was serious, and he dispatched to meet it Mahone's infantry division and two cavalry divisions — Hampton's and Rooney Lee's. He also recalled Fitzhugh Lee's cavalry division from Culpeper.

Hancock decided to shift the weight of his attack farther to the north, in an attempt to turn the Confederate left. During the night he had Birney pull back most of his command and march it behind Mott's and Barlow's divisions toward the extreme Federal right. Birney was to complete his circuit and attack the enemy flank as early as possible on August 15, while Gregg launched a diversionary attack up the Charles City road.

But Birney fell victim to a different enemy — the thick, brushy, vine-clustered woods of the Tidewater. Getting through this tangle, on terrain that was flat and devoid of landmarks, along narrow, winding paths, would have been difficult enough for an individual who was familiar with the area. For an army led by newcomers with inadequate maps, the task was nearly impossible.

For the entire day on August 15, Birney and X Corps virtually disappeared, groping toward the enemy left. It was after 6 p.m. before they found their bearings and, by that time, too late to attack.

Early the next morning, Gregg's cavalry and one of Barlow's infantry brigades fought their way to within seven miles of the Confederate capital, driving off an enemy cavalry brigade and killing its commander, Brigadier General John R. Chambliss Jr. At 10 a.m. Birney launched his assault at Fussell's Mill, the skirmishers fighting their way forward through a huckleberry swamp and heavy undergrowth.

Confederate Colonel William C. Oates (*right foreground*) directs the 15th and the 48th Alabama in a successful repulse of Hancock's corps at Fussell's Mill on August 16. Later that day, a Minié ball struck Oates in the shoulder, a wound that necessitated the amputation of his right arm.

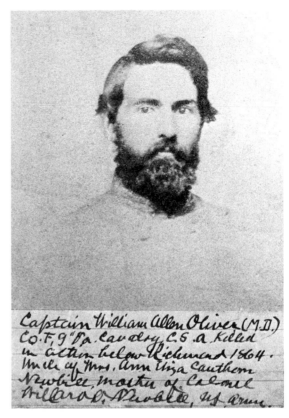

Captain William Allen Oliver (M.D.) Co. F, 9th Va. Cavalry, C.S.a Killed in action below Richmond 1864. Uncle of Mrs. Ann Eliza Cauthorn Newbill, mother of Colonel Millard D. Newbill, US Army.

Overcoming the difficulties, X Corps hit the enemy line hard, and now the Confederates showed that the stress of the long campaign was affecting them as well. Two of Field's brigades broke and ran, opening a perilous gap in the center of the Confederate line. As Field wrote later, "Not only the day but Richmond seemed to be gone."

Neither Birney nor Hancock, however, could see his advantage through the brush. Hancock later complained, "It was several hours before I could ascertain the exact state of affairs." By then it was too late. Field had brought in additional brigades from his left — despite the threat posed there by Gregg — and from his right and sent them against the newly taken works. At first the Confederates were driven back; but while they regrouped, their wounded comrades lying between the lines shouted to them to charge again. "Enthusiasm seized the whole line," recalled Captain James F. J. Caldwell of the 1st South Carolina. "With a yell they dashed against the fortifications, stormed out the dense line crowded there, and killed them by the scores as they fled."

About the same time, Hampton's Confederate riders slammed into Gregg's cavalry and drove it back with heavy casualties. The Federal rear guard, about to be overrun, retreated for safety into a swamp.

It was clear to Hancock that he was facing a great deal more resistance — five confederate divisions, about 20,000 men in all — than he had anticipated. With his force of 28,000, he was not going to be able to dislodge an entrenched enemy and gain Richmond. The Federals had already suffered nearly 3,000 casualties, three times the defenders' losses.

Grant was unperturbed by the situation. He told Hancock to stay where he was, threatening and skirmishing but not attempting to attack the enemy lines. Then Grant told Meade that it was time to strike again with the other fist, south of the James.

Preparations for this move began on August 14, the day Hancock had advanced from Deep Bottom. That night, General Warren started pulling V Corps out of the line on the Federal left. Its place was taken by Burnside's old IX Corps, now commanded by Major General John G. Parke. The corps simply extended to the left, increasing the intervals between men until the gap in the line was covered. After waiting to see how Hancock fared, Grant sent Warren forward on the morning of August 18.

Grant had several reasons for ordering the move, but the primary one, as before, was to sever another of Lee's lines of supply — this time the Weldon Railroad. Warren was to cut it as close to the enemy lines as possible, then destroy it as far south as he could safely go. "I do not want him to fight any unequal battles or to assault fortifications," Grant said. But Warren was told to consider his

The marshy expanse of White Oak swamp blocked the retreat of the Federal cavalry's rear guard from Fussell's Mill. "A few escaped capture," a trooper wrote, "but none a submersion, head and ears, in the foul-smelling ooze into which they and their steeds sank."

Sergeant Solomon Miller (*near right*) and Private Henry Baker of the 76th Pennsylvania, a unit known as the Keystone Zouaves, took part in the unsuccessful Federal charge on Lee's defenses at Deep Bottom, Virginia, on August 16. Private Baker was killed in the action.

mission a reconnaissance in force and to take advantage of any weakness he discovered.

Rain had come at last to southern Virginia, but instead of bringing relief from the heat it merely raised the humidity — and turned the roads to quagmires. Warren marched his men west at 4 a.m. on the 18th, but they were slowed by the struggle to haul their wagons and artillery through the mud: After three hours they had advanced only about two miles. At that point they met and brushed aside a Confederate cavalry brigade, and by 9 a.m., they had reached the railroad at Globe Tavern, just three miles south of the Confederate fortifications around Petersburg.

General Warren established his headquarters at the tavern and deployed his 10,000 men. Brigadier General Charles Griffin's 1st Division went to work tearing up track while the 2nd Division, under the leadership of

Brigadier General Romeyn B. Ayres, moved north to stand guard. Brigadier General Samuel W. Crawford's 3rd Division took up its position on Ayres's right, and Brigadier General Lysander Cutler's 4th Division was held in reserve to the rear.

The Confederate cavalry had reported that a Federal force was astride the Weldon Railroad. General Beauregard, who was back in command at Petersburg while Lee was north of the river, immediately dispatched Major General Henry Heth to the south with two brigades. Advancing through thick woods, Heth slashed into General Ayres's left flank at 2 p.m. He caught Colonel Nathan T. Dushane's Maryland brigade by surprise, and the Federals fell back in confusion. Within minutes, Colonel Joseph Hayes's brigade also was in retreat.

But Ayres proved to be equal to the emergency. Quickly, he brought forward his reserves, rallied the scattered troops and, with aid from Cutler's and Crawford's divisions, launched a counterattack. By nightfall the Federals had regained their original position. Their casualties exceeded 900, and those of the Confederates were presumed to be about the same.

Meade was delighted with the progress Warren had made, and he sent word that the railroad must be held "at all hazards." Then he set about getting Warren some help. On August 19, one of Hancock's divisions was recalled from Deep Bottom to help IX Corps and XVIII Corps extend their lines even more; this freed three IX Corps divisions, which were sent to Globe Tavern.

Warren, in the meantime, ordered Brigadier General Edward S. Bragg, commanding the battered remnant of the famed Iron Brigade, to extend the V Corps line to the right

A Photograph without a Camera

The death of Confederate General John R. Chambliss Jr. on August 16 set off an unusual race against time. Chambliss fell while leading a cavalry charge at Deep Bottom. When his body was recovered by a former West Point classmate, Union General David M. Gregg, it yielded an unexpected treasure: a map that showed in detail the defenses of Richmond.

Gregg turned the map over to the Topographical Engineers, who recognized that, to make maximum use of its contents, the map had to be copied and distrib-

uted more rapidly than they could possibly do by hand. The mapmakers decided to try Margedant's Quick Method. This new photographic process, developed by Captain W. C. Margedant of the 9th Ohio, had an extraordinary feature: It

required no camera. Instead, a tracing of Chambliss' map was laid over a sheet of photographic paper and exposed to the sun. The sun's rays darkened the photographic paper except under the ink lines of the tracing, producing a photocopy negative in which roads, rivers and other map features appeared as white lines against a dark background.

The new technique proved fast and effective. Within 48 hours of Chambliss' death, every Federal commander in the area had a copy of the map in his hands.

GENERAL JOHN R. CHAMBLISS JR.

GENERAL DAVID M. GREGG

and make a connection with IX Corps's left. These lines were stretched thin, and the widely scattered men had to find each other in dense underbrush where visibility was limited to about 20 paces, then maintain contact and watch for the enemy. Bragg was slow to move, got lost in the woods and wound up behind General Crawford's line instead of on Crawford's right as planned.

By now, Confederate reinforcements were marching south across the river. Lee had detached Mahone's infantry division and Rooney Lee's cavalry to help retake the Weldon Railroad. At 4:15 p.m. on August 19 Mahone struck Warren's right flank at its weakest point — where Bragg's Iron Brigade was still trying to find its proper place in line. Bragg's troops gave way and Mahone surged ahead, punching a hole through Crawford's line and sweeping down on his flank and rear. "At this moment," Crawford later wrote, "our artillery opened fire upon friend and foe, the shells bursting among our men, the projectiles striking in the rear of the breastworks." Caught between two fires, hundreds of Crawford's men fled in panic and the V Corps line began to crumble from right to left.

Crawford galloped among his scattered soldiers in a vain effort to stem the rout. Four of the general's staff officers had their horses shot from under them, as did the soldier who carried the headquarters flag; Crawford's orderly was killed, and the general himself narrowly escaped capture. In all, the better part of two brigades surrendered to Mahone's victorious Confederates.

Meanwhile, Heth had launched a frontal assault against Warren's center and left. Ayres's division stoutly withstood this onslaught, and General Warren re-formed the routed elements of his right wing. With this force and the arriving divisions from IX Corps, Warren counterattacked through the thickets, regaining his line in savage, hand-to-hand fighting. Mahone's division was sent reeling all the way to the fortifications, carrying along some of the Federal units that had become entangled with it.

General Heth remained on the field with his two brigades; he hit Ayres's front again and again, but he could not uproot him. As night fell, Warren retained possession of the field, Globe Tavern, his original line and, most important, the Weldon Railroad. He had lost only 382 killed and wounded, but more than 2,500 of his men, including 1,800 from Crawford's division, were missing and presumed captured.

The next day, while continuing with the destruction of the railroad, Warren pulled his men out of the maddening underbrush and ordered them to establish a new line about two miles to the rear, on open ground where they could see the enemy and bring their guns to bear. Drenched by a pouring rain, the exhausted soldiers labored through the night, and by dawn they had erected formidable earthworks.

The wisdom of Warren's move was confirmed that day, August 21, when both Mahone and A. P. Hill assaulted his line. The Confederates charged three ranks deep, screaming as they came. Warren galloped along the line, shouting: "Fire low! Low! Low!" The 26 guns of Colonel Charles Wainwright's artillery brigade opened up, cutting great swaths in the approaching ranks. As Wainwright wrote that evening, "Their yell was stopped in their throats before it was well out."

Hill decided to call off the attack; but

through a mistake in orders, Brigadier General Johnson Hagood's South Carolina brigade continued the charge against the Federal left. Hagood, a combative prewar Secessionist, managed to drive some troops of Lysander Cutler's 4th Division from their breastworks. But as the disorganized attackers pressed on, they were caught in a deadly crossfire. Those South Carolinians who were not killed or wounded began to throw down their weapons and surrender to the Federals, who came swarming out of their entrenchments.

Hagood himself was approached by one of Cutler's staff officers, Captain Dennis Dailey, who carried a captured Confederate flag. Rather than surrender, however, Hagood shot Dailey, seized the flag and rode off on the wounded Federal's horse. Before the startled Union troops could react, many of Hagood's men also bolted to the rear. Even so, 448 of Hagood's 681 men were dead, wounded or captured, and six flags remained in Federal hands.

The Federal hold on the Weldon Railroad was secure, and now began the work of extending the fortifications and the entrenchments. Soon Globe Tavern was knitted firmly into the Federal works, and Petersburg was half encircled. The noose around the neck of Lee's army had been drawn a little tighter.

Yet not tight enough, by far. Although the Federals had cut the railroad, the Confederates continued to use it. They simply stopped their trains a day's ride south of the enemy, transferred their goods to wagons and hauled them around the Federal left into Petersburg. "Whilst we are inconvenienced," said a member of Lee's staff, "no material harm is done us."

Major General Henry Heth led two Confederate brigades against Warren's V Corps at the Weldon Railroad on August 19. Heth's force was unable to dislodge the stubborn Federals: "I drove them from two lines of breastworks," he wrote, "but could do no more."

Grant was determined that more harm be done. The railroad had to be destroyed farther to the south, and he gave the job to Hancock, who on the 21st had just completed an exhausting march back to the main Federal lines from Deep Bottom. The men of II Corps were becoming known as "Hancock's Cavalry"; they stopped marching, it was said, only while the staff officers got fresh horses.

Without pausing to rest, Hancock set two of his divisions to their new task. With Gregg's cavalry screening for them, they began tearing up mile after mile of the Weldon tracks, working south from Warren's lines. By the evening of August 24, having destroyed eight miles of track, they bivouacked at Reams's Station, five miles south of Globe Tavern, where some half-completed earthworks had been thrown up in June.

That evening, signalmen reported to Meade that a large number of Confederates, perhaps 10,000, were moving out of their lines toward the southwest. They were obviously going to attack either Warren or Hancock, and Meade alerted both commanders.

Hancock was the target. Lee wanted the

Weldon Railroad back, and he had given the assignment to A. P. Hill. It was Hill's corps, along with Hampton's two cavalry divisions, that the Federal signalmen had spotted.

The next morning, August 25, Hancock cautiously sent his cavalry out on reconnaissance. Gregg's riders found only the usual detachments of Rooney Lee's cavalry, which had been harassing the Federals all along; Gregg reported that there was no large enemy force in the area. On hearing this at noon, Hancock ordered John Gibbon, just back from leave, to take his division south and resume the destruction of the railroad.

Gibbon's men had just started out when the Federal cavalry pickets west of the railroad were attacked and driven in. Assuming this was to be just another annoying skirmish, Gregg deployed his cavalry to deal with it, but the troopers soon ran into Confederate infantry. Gregg was confronting more firepower than he could handle, and the enemy units broke through his line to the Federal left and rear. With help from Gibbon, Gregg eventually drove the Confederates back to the west, and for a time the fighting ended — it had been a reconnaissance, not a full-scale attack.

But Hancock knew that an attack was coming and that his situation was perilous. He had taken prisoners from no fewer than three Confederate divisions, and the temporary breakthrough had shown how easily his force might be cut off from the rest of the

Major General Gouverneur K. Warren (*fifth from left*) stands with his staff before their headquarters flag, which bears the Maltese cross insignia of the Federal V Corps. During their raids on the Weldon Railroad, the men of V Corps delighted in forming rough Maltese crosses from sections of heated rails.

AUGUST 18TH

BATTERY H, 1ST N.Y. BATTERY B, 1ST N.Y. BATTERY D, 5TH U.S. 5TH N.Y. REGT.

DRAWN BY R.HOLLAND.

Genl R. B. Ayres or

BATTLE OF THE WELDON

AUGUST 21ST 1864.

106

AUGUST 19TH

18TH MAINE REGT.

J. H. BUFFORDS' LITH. BOSTON.

L-ROAD.

army. Hancock ordered Gibbon's division back into the earthworks at Reams's Station. The works formed three sides of a square, each side roughly 1,000 yards long, with the open end on the east. Gibbon took the left, or southern, half while the right was manned by Barlow's division, now commanded by Brigadier General Nelson A. Miles. (Barlow, whose health had failed after the fight at Fussell's Mill, had been carried from Reams's Station on a stretcher.)

At 2 p.m., a pair of Confederate brigades attacked Miles's line. They were repulsed, yet they left dead and wounded men lying within a few yards of the Federal breastworks. In the meantime, the Confederates were massing for a larger assault under Major General Wilcox — A. P. Hill also having been incapacitated by illness.

In midafternoon Hancock received word from Meade that plenty of help was on the way: Hancock's own 3rd Division under Gershom Mott and an additional IX Corps division. But instead of marching five miles straight south from Globe Tavern, these reinforcements had been sent on a circuitous 12-mile route that approached Reams's Station from the south. It would be several hours before they were available.

At 5 p.m., Hill's batteries, under 23-year-old Lieutenant Colonel William Johnson Pegram, opened a furious barrage on the Federal trenches. Pegram's fire caused few casualties, but it seriously demoralized the large number of draftees and recruits in II Corps, many of whom had never been in combat before. The shelling especially panicked the men on the west and south sides of the rectangle, which were enfiladed and even taken in the rear by the enemy cannon. In order to escape the fire, some of Gibbon's

107

men sought shelter outside their earthworks.

After a quarter-hour bombardment, six Confederate brigades of Heth's and Wilcox's divisions launched their assault, once again at Miles's division on Hancock's right. And now, after so many engagements in which Federal infantrymen had fought better than their officers deserved, two of the best officers in the Army of the Potomac — Miles and Hancock — were let down by their men.

At first the Confederate advance was staggered by the concentrated fire from Miles's division. "Men who seemed to have possessed charmed lives were struck down almost in a body," recalled Captain John Thorp of the 47th North Carolina. But just when it looked as though the attack would be repulsed, two regiments in the center of Miles's line fled from their breastworks. Miles ordered Colonel Horace Rugg's brigade up from reserve to close the gap, but to his astonishment Rugg's men fell prone and refused to open fire.

Major Charles Stedman of the 44th North Carolina said the Federals "seemed to be dazed by the vehemence of the attack." They fired wildly into the air and offered little resistance once the Southern troops gained the works. General Heth led the Confederate charge in person, against his prewar Army friend, Hancock. In his enthusiasm, Heth at one point tried to snatch the flag from the hands of color-bearer Thomas Minton of the 26th North Carolina. "I won't surrender up my colors," Minton shouted. "Come on then," Heth answered. "We will carry the colors together." Soon the gap in the Federal line widened, and the attackers began rolling up the defenders on either side.

When the Confederates broke through the Union entrenchments on the right of Lieutenant Henry Granger's 10th Massachusetts Battery, the artillerists stuck to their guns. They had little choice: All but one of the battery's horses had fallen to enemy fire. Granger wheeled the right-hand gun, fired a load of canister into the oncoming North Carolinians of Brigadier General William McRae's brigade, then scrambled to the next gun, and so on down the line, sending the deadly charge of iron balls tearing through the ranks of his assailants. But Granger's bravery was to no avail; within minutes all four guns were in Confederate hands.

Hancock was face to face with disaster, and he knew it. Disregarding his own safety, he galloped from point to threatened point, railing at his men to stand fast, until suddenly his horse dropped under him. Hancock left the animal for dead, but a few minutes later it clambered to its feet, unharmed by a glancing blow to the spine that had temporarily paralyzed it. Hancock remounted and continued the fight. "We can beat them yet," he bellowed. "Don't leave me, for God's sake!"

Hancock ordered Gibbon to retake the trenches and guns from the enemy, but Gibbon's division, part of which had already been rolled up on the right, flinched from the task. They were being fired on, albeit lightly, from the right and rear and stayed huddled in the ditches behind their breastworks. Hancock was mortified by the sorry performance of his once-proud corps. "I do not care to die," he told a colonel during the battle. "But I pray God I may never leave this field."

Now only General Miles stood between II Corps and catastrophe. While his staff officers tried desperately to rally the fleeing infantrymen, Miles ordered Lieutenant

For General Winfield Scott Hancock, the battle at Reams's Station was the "blackest of all days" in the history of II Corps, despite the general's personal bravery. "Hancock had his bridle-rein cut by a bullet," wrote an admiring soldier, "but was continually galloping along the front urging the stragglers to resume their places in the lines and do their duty."

led it back to his original line and beyond, moving in front of the Federal works to sweep along the entrenchments, driving out the enemy and recapturing Dauchy's guns. Gibbon's officers tried to get some of the 2nd Division troops on their feet to help in this effort, but again the men refused to move.

Earlier, Wade Hampton had withdrawn his Confederate cavalry divisions, apparently leaving the fight. In reality, however, Hampton had been moving around to Hancock's left. There he had his men dismount, and just as Miles was starting to succeed with his counterattack, Hampton's men struck Gibbon's left flank. The Federals, now completely unnerved, deserted their entrenchments and fell back.

General Gregg, who with the exception of Miles had the only Federal force on the field that was still functioning, was guarding the left. He dismounted his men and fired into Hampton's flank, stopping the Confederate advance. But when Hampton's two divisions turned their full attention to Gregg, the latter was forced to join his line with Gibbon's, some distance behind the entrenchments.

The Federals could not stay where they were — in the open without breastworks. They must either retake their fortifications or withdraw. Miles and Gregg wanted to attack, but Gibbon confessed that his division was not up to it. Having lost almost 2,400 casualties (2,150 of whom had been taken prisoner) and nine guns, with no sign of the promised reinforcements, Hancock gave the order to pull out after dark.

Orlando Willcox's IX Corps division arrived in time to act as a rear guard for the retreat, which went smoothly because the Confederates did not try to follow up their

George K. Dauchy to swing the three Napoleon guns of his 12th New York Battery around to face the Southerners pouring through the gap on his left. Dauchy had already lost one cannon to the attackers and was eager for revenge. As a column of Confederate troops neared his guns, Dauchy gave the command to fire, and a triple charge of canister mowed down the leading ranks. Within minutes, the battery was overrun, but in the time thus bought, Miles had managed to rally the 61st New York Infantry. He

success. "Had our troops behaved as they used to I could have beaten Hill," Hancock told Willcox that night. "But some were new, and all were worn out with labor." Willcox wrote later that Hancock had never looked better, and the withdrawal "was more like abdication than defeat."

But more had been lost that day than a position; the invincible II Corps had collapsed, losing 12 battle flags despite the best efforts of the commander they called "Hancock the Superb." "The agony of that day never passed away from that proud soldier, who, for the first time, saw his lines broken and his guns taken," wrote Hancock's chief of staff, Colonel Charles H. Morgan.

Gibbon later tried to explain to his corps commander why his division had behaved so badly. Among other reasons, he pointed out that in four months his four brigades had lost nine brigade and 40 regimental commanders, with the result that sergeants were leading companies and captains, regiments.

Hancock was so unsympathetic that Gibbon considered himself insulted and offered to resign. There were heated exchanges and unfortunate accusations. Both men calmed down eventually, Hancock taking back his harsh words and Gibbon his resignation. But their close friendship was over. Soon both would leave the corps that had been at the center of their lives for so long. "The glory of the division," Gibbon lamented — and he might well have included the corps and its commander — "was in the past."

However devastating the affair at Reams's Station had been to Hancock and II Corps, Grant was entirely satisfied. Lee's men were hungry, and without the Weldon Railroad they would get hungrier still; they were spread too thin along their fortifications, and now they had to extend their lines even farther to cover the Federal threat from the south. Already weary, they continually had to dash north, then south, of the James to parry vicious Federal threats they could not see coming until almost too late. Above all, Lee needed more men. "Unless some measures can be devised to replace our losses," he warned the Confederate Secretary of War, "the consequences may be disastrous."

As confident as Grant remained, he understood that his army, too, was almost used up. Moreover, there were fortifications to extend along his newly gained positions, and for these reasons he put a stop to offensive operations for almost a month.

Brigadier General Nelson A. Miles staved off a total rout at Reams's Station by rallying survivors of the battered 61st New York to recapture a battery and a portion of the Federal line. "Miles threw the 61st across the breastworks at right angles," wrote a witness, "and commenced to fight his way back, leading the regiment in person."

During this period of comparative rest, which was sorely needed by both sides, Lee urged General Hampton to look for a chance to strike at Grant's headquarters and supply base at City Point, eight miles northeast of Petersburg, at the confluence of the Appomattox and the James. "I judge that the enemy is very open to attack at City Point," Lee wrote to his cavalry chief on September 3. "A sudden blow in that quarter might be detrimental to him."

Two days later Hampton received a report from one of his best scouts, Sergeant George Shadburne, whose camp was hidden along the Blackwater River, two miles behind Grant's lines. "I have just returned from City Point," Shadburne announced. He described the activities and defenses of the Federal supply base and added: "At Coggins' Point are 3,000 beeves, attended by 120 men, and 30 citizens without arms." That

many beef cattle, if Hampton could abduct them, would provide Lee's entire army a daily meat ration for at least six weeks.

Coggins' Point was on the James about five miles below City Point. The only substantial body of armed men that Shadburne could find near the herd was a 250-man detachment from the 1st District of Columbia Cavalry at Sycamore Church, three miles south of the cattle. The greatest danger to Confederate raiders, said Shadburne, would come on their way back when they had to take the Jerusalem Plank Road, close to an enemy that by then would be alarmed.

His interest aroused, Hampton told Shadburne to investigate further, asking if Grant was expected to be away from the army any time soon. Shadburne responded that Grant would be going to the Shenandoah Valley to see Sheridan on September 14.

Assuming that a raid would have a better chance of success with the enemy commander absent, Hampton asked Lee for permission to try it. He proposed to take 4,500 troopers on an arduous 100-mile ride, much of it behind Federal lines; they would leave September 14. Lee approved, warning Hampton only to be careful.

From their position on the right flank of the Confederate lines south of Petersburg,

the raiders started out early on the 14th, riding straight south all that day and part of the next. Then, guided by Sergeant Shadburne, they turned northeast and made for Cook's Bridge on Blackwater River, four miles in the rear of the Federal IX Corps and 10 miles from Coggins' Point.

Cook's Bridge had been destroyed, as Hampton well knew; he chose it as a crossing point because the enemy would not be watching it closely. He came prepared, and while his troopers dismounted to rest, his engineers went to work erecting a new bridge. They finished the job before dark.

The men had a cold camp that evening. As deep in enemy territory as they were, they could not light campfires. They found some sweet potatoes, hungrily dug them up and chewed on them raw as they crossed the new bridge at midnight.

Thus far the men had not known where they were going or why, but now the orders were laid out. General Rooney Lee was to take his division to the left, placing it between the cattle herd and Grant's army. He was to prevent news of the raid from reaching the Federals for as long as possible and then act as rear guard. Brigadier General James Dearing's brigade was to move on the right, protecting that flank, while Hamp-

111

Digging a Shortcut to Richmond

In midsummer of 1864, after an embarrassing month spent bottled up at Bermuda Hundred, General Benjamin Butler devised another of his many plans to take the city of Richmond — this time by water. For several months, Confederate batteries had dominated a strategic section of the James River at Trent Reach, blocking the passage of Federal gunboats. Navigation was further impeded by obstructions that Butler himself had sunk into the river during an earlier retreat.

Butler's scheme involved cutting a canal across a 174-yard neck of land called Dutch Gap, bypassing nearly five miles of the meandering river controlled by the Confederates. Digging began on August 10 and continued until December 30. On the 31st, the bulkhead at the north end of the canal was blown out with a 12,000-pound charge of powder. Steam dredges then moved in to complete the excavation. The canal was not opened to river traffic until April of 1865 — too late to be of any military value. After the War, however, Butler's Dutch Gap Canal became the customary channel for shipping on the James.

Working within range of Confederate artillery, laborers cut a canal 43 yards wide across Dutch Gap, which was intended to allow Federal gunboats to operate against the Confederate capital of Richmond. The completed channel *(inset)* required the excavation of nearly 67,000 cubic yards of dirt.

136 °] Nov. 19, 1864.]

THE ADVANCE AGAINST RICHMOND—PROGRESS OF WORK ON DUTCH GA

GEN. BUTLER'S DEPARTMENT—CUTTING THROUGH PENINSULA, TO AVOID REBEL OBSTRUCTIONS AND SHORTEN THE ROUTE OF OUR GUNBOATS TO RICHMOND.

Cattle Raid
A. R. Ward

ton himself, with Brigadier General Thomas Rosser's brigade and a battalion led by Lieutenant Colonel Lovick P. Miller, headed straight for Coggins' Point and the herd.

First, Rosser would have to deal with the Federal cavalrymen at Sycamore Church. At first light he drove in their pickets and confronted their main body, waiting behind hastily built breastworks. Rosser's force outnumbered the Federals 10 to 1. But when Rosser demanded their surrender, the response was: "Come and get us if you want us." The Confederates opened fire, and although the 1st D.C. Cavalry fought back gamely, the shooting was over in a few minutes. After taking prisoner almost the entire 250-man Federal contingent, Hampton and

Rosser hurried on toward Coggins' Point.

Captain Nathaniel Richardson, the Commissary of Subsistence in charge of the Federal herd, had spent a quiet night. He and his herdsmen had bedded down the cattle earlier than usual that evening, yet most of the animals were still lying down in their corral when he arose. Then, just before 5 a.m., Richardson received an urgent message from Captain Henry Gregg of the 13th Pennsylvania, the commander of his small cavalry guard. Gregg's pickets had been attacked.

Richardson roused his herdsmen. He had just ordered them to tear down the fence and scatter the cattle when he heard the fearsome howls of a Rebel charge. Hampton's men seemed to come out of nowhere and were all

Cracking their whips, Confederate cavalrymen led by Major General Wade Hampton (*right*) drive homeward the 2,486 head of cattle captured on their so-called beefsteak raid behind Federal lines. Flushed with success and heedless of pursuing Federals, the raiders paused long enough to present a steer to a farmgirl they passed along the way.

around him at once, the 1st D.C. and 13th Pennsylvania Cavalries fleeing before them.

"I saw that all was lost," Richardson said later. He and his men ran for their lives. Only 20 steers escaped before the Confederates surrounded the herd. By 6 a.m., with the help of several shepherd dogs they had brought along, the raiders had the cattle well in hand and were on their way back toward Blackwater River. Rooney Lee and his division remained behind for three hours to cover the withdrawal. Now Hampton sent Rosser ahead several miles to the Jerusalem Plank Road, where the Federals would most likely try to intercept him. Rosser was to take a position on the road and hold it so the cattle could be driven across behind him.

Hampton had forded the Blackwater with the cattle and was nearing the plank road when Rosser reported the approach of Federal troopers. Ordering Rosser to hold his ground, Hampton turned the herd farther to the south and drove it toward the Nottoway River. No sooner had the animals crossed the river than pursuing Federal cavalry under General August Kautz caught up with Rosser and attacked. Dearing and Rooney Lee hurried to Rosser's aid, and together the Confederates held off the Federals until after midnight, when Kautz gave up the effort.

Hampton bivouacked safely that night, and the next day he herded his prize into the Confederate camp, proudly turning over 2,468 steers to the army commissary. Only 18 animals had been lost on the drive home.

A few more cattle were lost to the raiders themselves, however. That night the cavalry dined lavishly on steaks and on sardines taken from captured Yankee wagons. They had much to celebrate. At a cost of 10 men killed and 47 wounded, Hampton had taken the cattle, 11 wagons heavily laden with supplies and 304 prisoners. A few days later, when General Grant was asked when he expected to starve Lee out of Richmond, he replied: "Never, if our armies continue to supply him with beef-cattle."

The Confederate troopers would not soon forget their exploit, nor would they let Billy Yank forget it. During a battle two weeks later, some of Hampton's men were seen standing on breastworks and shouting across the lines, "Good fat beef over here, come over and get some." Then, for once withholding their Rebel yell, the Confederates were heard gleefully "bellowing like bulls."

The Grim Testing of Black Troops

The banner carried by the 22nd Regiment U.S. Colored Troops pictures a bayonet-wielding black soldier overpowering a Confederate. The Latin motto at top, meaning "Thus Always to Tyrants," had an ironic thrust; it was also the state motto of slaveholding Virginia.

Charging at the run, men of the 22nd U.S. Colored Troops capture a Confederate entrenchment on the Dimmock Line outside Petersburg on June 16, 1864. One of the unit's officers wrote afterward, "I never saw troops fight better, more bravely, and with more determination and enthusiasm."

More black soldiers, totaling 38 regiments, served with the Union armies besieging Petersburg and Richmond than in any other Civil War campaign. In that grim crucible they erased the doubts about their fighting ability that had been harbored by Grant and other Federal generals — and by white troops on both sides. Blacks fought desperately in the chaos of the Battle of the Crater, one brigade suffering 1,324 casualties, and later they took the lead in assaults on New Market Heights and other Confederate strongholds. For individual gallantry in these attacks, 23 black soldiers earned the Congressional Medal of Honor.

One Medal of Honor winner, Sergeant Major Christian Fleetwood, wrote later that his fellow blacks fought so well because they felt intensely the need to prove their bravery to the world. They "stood in the full glare of the greatest searchlight, part and parcel of the grandest armies ever mustered on this continent," Fleetwood said, competing "with the bravest and the best" and "losing nothing by comparison."

Fiery Baptism in the Crater

Soldiers of the 23rd U.S. Colored Troops dash into the huge crater created by an exploded mine on July 30, 1864, reinforcing a Massachusetts brigade trapped there by Confederate fire. This was their first major battle, but the infantrymen fought stubbornly and the best of them were repulsed, an officer said, only "when the enemy's banners waved in their faces."

Sergeant Andrew Davis of the 29th U.S. Colored Troops, which also fought in the Battle of the Crater, survived the bloody repulse although his regiment lost 20 percent of its men in minutes when bungling Federal commanders turned the Crater into a death trap for the attackers.

Settling In for the Siege

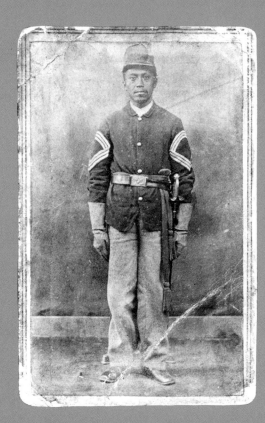

Charles Springer of the 107th U.S. Colored Troops proudly wears the chevrons of a sergeant major, a rank he earned during the long Petersburg siege. Sergeant major was the highest rank attained by blacks during the War; the commissioned officers in charge of their units were white.

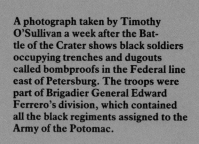

A photograph taken by Timothy O'Sullivan a week after the Battle of the Crater shows black soldiers occupying trenches and dugouts called bombproofs in the Federal line east of Petersburg. The troops were part of Brigadier General Edward Ferrero's division, which contained all the black regiments assigned to the Army of the Potomac.

The bullet-torn headquarters flag of the 1st Brigade of Ferrero's black division attests to the heavy fire the raw recruits faced in the Crater. Said the brigade commander, Colonel Joshua Sigfried, it was "hot enough to cause the oldest of troops to falter."

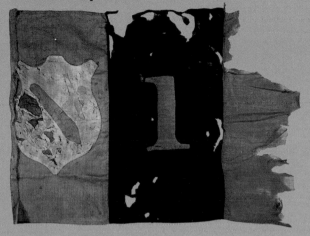

White soldiers join blacks in a photograph taken at Point of Rocks, a Federal supply depot on the Appomattox River. Such fraternization was fairly rare, even though many whites recognized that blacks had proved to be first-rate troops.

Two dozen survivors of a company in the 4th U.S. Colored Troops stand at rest while serving guard duty near Washington after the War. Their regiment lost 178 men killed or wounded in the Federal attacks on Fort Harrison. "When we were ordered to do our duty," one of them wrote, "we went like men."

Costly Repulses and a Successful Charge

Lieutenant Charles Teeple, a white officer in the 7th U.S. Colored Troops, prepares a casualty report after his unit's futile assault on Fort Gilmer. In the two days of fighting at New Market Heights, the 7th lost half of its men.

Massed Federal forces, including four companies of the 7th U.S. Colored Troops, surge across fireswept ground toward Fort Gilmer (*background*) on September 30. The black troops advanced — at a cost of 61 men — to the fort's ramparts, where only a few escaped being killed or captured.

Honors for Exceptional Courage

MILTON M. HOLLAND
Sergeant Major
5th U.S.C.T.

The Medal of Honor, the nation's highest award for valor *(right)*, was awarded to no fewer than 13 black soldiers who took part in the New Market Heights attacks; seven of those honored are shown here. Perhaps the most remarkable among them was Sergeant Alexander Kelly, seen as an elderly man below, right, who advanced with his regiment's colors after virtually all of the color guard had been cut down. So notable was the courage of the black troops that General Benjamin Butler was moved to write: "I felt in my inmost heart that the capacity of the Negro race for soldiers had then and there been fully settled forever."

JAMES H. HARRIS
Sergeant
38th U.S.C.T.

ALEXANDER KELLY
First Sergeant
6th U.S.C.T.

CHRISTIAN A. FLEETWOOD
Sergeant Major
4th U.S.C.T.

JAMES GARDINER
Private
36th U.S.C.T.

ROBERT A. PINN
First Sergeant
5th U.S.C.T.

POWHATAN BEATY
First Sergeant
5th U.S.C.T.

125

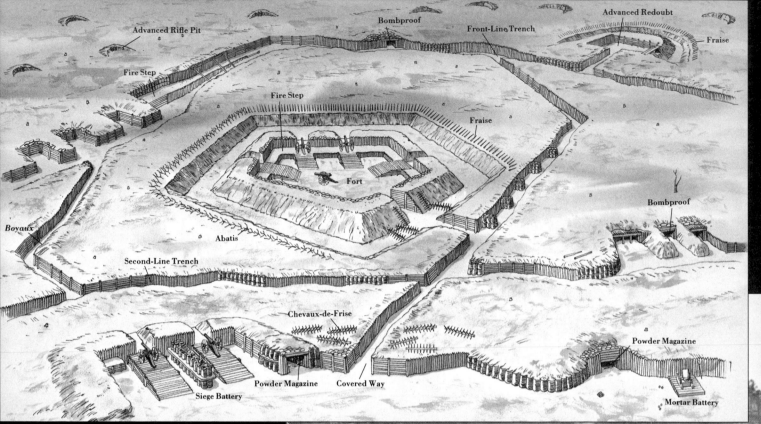

Advanced Rifle Pit

Fire Step

Bombproof

Front-Line Trench

Advanced Redoubt

Fraise

Fire Step

Fraise

Fort

Bombproof

Boyaux

Abatis

Second-Line Trench

Chevaux-de-Frise

Powder Magazine

Siege Battery

Powder Magazine

Covered Way

Mortar Battery

This diagram illustrates in condensed form the main elements of the entrenchments used by both armies at Petersburg. There were no fixed dimensions for the earthen walls or parapets, though experience had shown that 10 to 15 feet of earth would stop the heaviest artillery shell. A thickness of two feet was sufficient to stop a rifle shot.

Fraises, sharpened stakes angled to slow an enemy attack, jut from the rampart of Fort Sedgwick at the

Anatomy of a Trench System

The miles of entrenchments around Petersburg in 1864, which reminded one Federal soldier of "an immense prairie dog village," were based on established military principles, honed by three years of war. The works consisted of a series of low-lying forts like the one at left, connected by trench lines that were often two or more rows deep. The lines were linked to positions in the rear by zigzagging communication trenches called *boyaux*. These fed into covered ways, deep-cut routes often protected by roofs made of logs and earth so that a wagon train could pass in safety within a few hundred yards of the enemy.

Inside the forts, officers and men lived in burrow-like dugouts called bombproofs. In front of the main lines, advanced rifle pits and picket posts served as early-warning points, and far to the rear elaborate emplacements housed the heavy artillery.

The works were a monument to hard labor. Where the soil was soft, a soldier could excavate six cubic yards of earth in a day. Productivity dropped sharply, however, in rocky soil or close to enemy lines, where the work had to be done at night. In one deep ditch on the Federal side, it took eight men to get a single shovelful of dirt to the top of the works — one digging and the others standing in niches cut into the bank and passing the earth upward. Yet few complained. As one officer explained: "Nothing in the world finds more willing workers than throwing up breastworks under the spur of hostile fire."

southern end of the Union line. The fort was designed by Major Washington A. Roebling, who would earn postwar fame for building the Brooklyn Bridge.

The Outer Lines of Defense

The barriers at right, chevaux-de-frise, were made of logs 10 to 12 feet long and eight to 10 inches in diameter, with sharpened stakes inserted through holes bored in the logs. The Confederates put them 50 to 100 yards in front of the trenches. "These structures had to be renewed frequently," a soldier recalled, "being actually cut to pieces by the bullets."

A Federal sentry stands guard on a path leading through the rifle pits in front of a captured Confederate earthwork known as Fort Mahone. The men in the pits were the eyes and ears of the fortifications, alert for any enemy activity.

Federal soldiers take aim through loopholes in a captured picket post made of gabions, basket-like cylinders made of wicker and filled with dirt.

A Stout Labyrinth of Ditches

Chimneys of scavenged brick are all that remained of the winter quarters of Federal mortar battery No. 14 on the Petersburg line when this picture was taken after the siege. The trench at center leads to Fort Morton, the earthworks visible on the horizon.

Traverses constructed at right angles to the trench lines protected the troops from enfilading fire. Here at Fort Sedgwick the revetments, or retaining walls, of the traverses are built of gabions.

A civilian peers warily into a crude shelter dug into a section of the Federal line. The constant repairs and changes in the fortifications caused one soldier to remark, "The lines in some places became involved labyrinths, nearly impassable at night to one not familiar with the locality."

Inside an Earthen Fort

A wall of dirt-filled gabions reinforced by logs and sandbags shields the fire step of this section of Fort Sedgwick. To protect sharpshooters, logs with a square loophole strengthened by a small iron plate on the exterior were added to the top of the wall at several points along the fire step.

A Federal soldier relaxes on a log bracing a dome-shaped bombproof. In some forts, crosspieces of timber or railroad iron, covered with three feet of earth, were placed from the bombproofs to the parapets at intervals of about 50 yards to protect men on duty from mortar shells and other artillery fire.

The panoramic view, below, of the interior of Fort Sedgwick reveals an intricate maze of bombproofs, traverses and trenches. Confederate entrenchments are visible in front of the treeline on the horizon.

Ordnance with a Long Reach

A detail of Federal soldiers stands at the entrance to a powder magazine dug into the parapet of Fort Brady, near Aiken's Landing on the James River. The underground chamber was covered by six feet of earth packed on top of logs and gabions. Both armies at Petersburg sheltered their magazines so well that none blew up, despite many direct hits.

Flanked by his gunners, Captain H. H. Pierce of the 1st Connecticut Heavy Artillery stands on the carriage of a 100-pounder Parrott rifle at Fort Brady. These big guns protected the Federal supply base against attacks by Confederate gunboats and ironclads and countered enemy shelling from nearby Drewry's Bluff.

Federal officers and men emplace 10-inch siege mortars at the Crow's Nest, near Dutch Gap on the James River. The stubby, 1,852-pound mortars could hurl an 87-pound projectile more than a mile.

Portents of an Arduous Winter

"The city is now being pressed by the enemy in a manner I have never before witnessed or expected."

GENERAL SAMUEL COOPER, ADJUTANT AND INSPECTOR GENERAL, CSA

There was a change in the War that September. It was not easy to sense in the trenches at Petersburg, but from several directions came a persistent drumbeat of news signaling the shift. A desperate August, in which both sides had seemed equally afflicted by losses, exhaustion and shortages, was followed by a September of growing hope — for the Union.

As the month began, Atlanta fell to General William T. Sherman; it was the North's first clear-cut victory of the year. But that distant triumph was perhaps less appreciated by the Army of the Potomac than was the fact that the railroad from City Point, Virginia, had been extended to the immediate rear of the Federal lines at Petersburg. Now the trenchbound Federals could count not only on regular meals but on such forgotten treats as watermelon and peaches as well. "We are beginning to live tolerably here," wrote Colonel Charles S. Wainwright, V Corps's chief of artillery, in his diary.

At midmonth, Philip Sheridan attacked Jubal Early's corps on Opequon Creek in the Shenandoah Valley and sent it "whirling through Winchester," as a jubilant telegram declared. Meanwhile at Petersburg, Colonel Wainwright noticed that Federal recruits were now more than making up for the army's losses. "There is every prospect," he wrote on September 21, "of the regiment soon being full to the maximum allowed by law, which it has never yet been."

The next day Sheridan slammed into Early's regrouped Confederates at Fisher's Hill and chased them up the Valley and into the mountains. At General Grant's order, the guns of the Army of the Potomac fired a 100-gun salute — into the enemy works.

It was a portent. One week later the lull along the Richmond-Petersburg line would come to a stunning end. Grant would resume his relentless, alternating attacks north and south of the James River, and the capital of the Confederacy would confront its greatest peril of the War.

But while the respite lasted, the men of both armies tried to get sorely needed rest, despite the constant feints and alarms of trench warfare. "We have no idea, when we turn in at night, that we will be permitted to 'sleep out our full sleep' until morning," a Virginia artilleryman wrote in September. "There is hardly an acre of ground from Richmond to Petersburg, or from the James to the Chickahominy, that we have not been over a dozen times." The soldier and his comrades knew every road and lane so well, he wrote, that they could "go anywhere on the darkest night without mishap." Often as not they found themselves slogging through mud and rain on the kind of march that caused another Confederate to observe, "This knocks the poetry out of war, don't it?"

Even when there was no nighttime action, sleep was intermittent at best because of the almost-constant artillery fire. Every two minutes or so, all day and all night, an unseen mortar or a siege gun thundered out, in

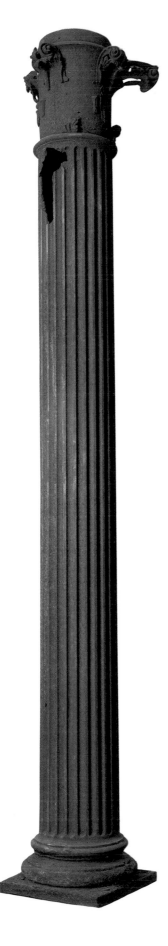

"The destructive work of the shells was visible on every hand," wrote a visitor to Petersburg in the summer of 1864. At left, scarred by Federal shellfire, is a cast-iron column, one of four that once graced the entrance to a library in Petersburg.

part simply to wear down the enemy by preventing sleep. The hard marching and lack of rest told heavily on the men. Another Virginia artilleryman, Major Robert A. Stiles, was appalled by the sight of one of General Mahone's infantry brigades when it came back from weeks of unrelieved service at the front. "We were shocked at the condition, the complexion, the expression of the men, and of the officers, too," he wrote. "Indeed we could scarcely realize that the unwashed, uncombed, unfed and almost unclad creatures we saw were officers of rank and reputation in the army."

Some of the men developed an eerie fascination for the agents of their destruction. "It is interesting to watch the flight of those shells," wrote Confederate Private Benjamin W. Jones of the Surry Light Artillery, "and to note the little cloud of white smoke that forms in the atmosphere where a shell explodes." The smoke formed a compact, round mass, Jones said, that "does not float off on the wind like any other cloud, but vanishes slowly from sight, a picture of all that is human."

While the men could never ignore the shelling entirely — "Often at night I jump up and run out expecting an attack," wrote one officer — they did learn to live with it. They also found ways to protect their sanity by having some fun. Men of the Federal Iron Brigade laid out a track for horse and mule races near their camp and enjoyed a good deal of sport until their corps commander, General Warren, ordered the track closed to enlisted men. Warren may have decided the diversion was causing the widespread lack of interest in clearing fields of fire and digging more trenches. "I never saw a lazier set of men in my life," he complained. Then he

added, with a touch of pride, "They are good for nothing but fighting."

Confederate soldiers sought relaxation in Petersburg and Richmond; the wounded and the furloughed filled the streets of both cities. At night, men slipped away from the trenches and went into town without permission — especially if there was a dance to attend. These informal soirees often were interrupted by an outbreak of shelling. Then the soldiers would go back to their works for an hour or so, recalled Lieutenant William M. Owen of the renowned Washington Artillery, "but not without securing a partner for a dance after their return."

In Richmond, soldiers and civilians continued the long-held custom of an evening promenade along Third Street to Gamble's Hill, where breezes on the height helped to soften the heat and humidity. Bands still played; girls still flirted. Often the young women came out to the front lines to ride the officers' horses or to stand daringly on the parapets and peer across at the Yankee soldiers sunning themselves. "Hello, Johnnie! It's ladies' day, ain't it?" a Federal sentinel would call out, and by unspoken agreement the pickets' firing would cease until the belles departed.

Remarkably, when the new Federal offensive came, it was initiated by the inept General Butler, at Bermuda Hundred. Since the Federal failure at Deep Bottom in August, Butler had been gathering information about the Confederate defenses. After the Weldon Railroad fighting of late August, Butler saw an opportunity in the weakness of the lines facing him north of the James and he prepared to grasp it.

The chance was even better than Butler

knew, for the Confederates were stretched dangerously thin. Lee, determined to regain the Weldon Railroad, had taken south to Petersburg all but three brigades of the Army of Northern Virginia. These three brigades, a brigade of cavalry and some reserve battalions from Richmond — fewer than 4,000 men — were all that stood between Butler's Army of the James and Richmond.

The Confederates did have a wealth of fortifications at their disposal. Three rows of Confederate entrenchments looped across the Peninsula, north of the James. The exterior and the intermediate lines were anchored on a fortified camp enclosing Chaffin's Bluff, with its vital river batteries and pontoon bridge. The interior line was a ring

of forts just outside Richmond. A fourth line, little more than a single trench, extended from Signal Hill below the camp to New Market Heights, five miles to the east.

To securely garrison these lines required more men than Lee had in his entire army. The defenders had to guess which sector was most threatened and go there, a task that was becoming more and more difficult as the men wore down. At the end of September, the few Confederates north of the James were concentrated at and around Chaffin's Bluff in the intermediate line and in the New Market line — which confronted the Federal position at Deep Bottom.

Butler proposed to hit the Confederates' New Market line and Chaffin's Bluff with a

Officers and crew surround the 13-inch mortar "Dictator," largest of the Federal guns plaguing Petersburg. Fired from a reinforced railroad car, the 17,000-pound weapon lofted its 200-pound shells up to two and a half miles. The shirt-sleeved gunners were commanded by Colonel Henry Abbot, seen standing in high boots beside the mortar.

three-pronged surprise attack. Major General Edward O. C. Ord would lead 8,000 men from XVIII Corps across the river at Aiken's Landing, two miles southwest of Deep Bottom. From there Ord would drive north along the Varina road, which passed in front of the eastern face of the works at Chaffin's Bluff. Ord was to assault Fort Harrison, the strong salient at the southeast corner of the camp, occupy Chaffin's Bluff and roll up the Confederate positions along the Osborne Turnpike toward Richmond.

Meanwhile, Major General David B. Birney with X Corps and Brigadier General Charles J. Paine's division of U.S. Colored Troops from XVIII Corps — 10,000 men in all — would advance from their position at Deep Bottom and surprise the Confederate left at New Market Heights. After Birney drove off the defenders, he was to move toward Richmond on the New Market road, which led to the northwest and eventually converged with the Osborne Turnpike. General Kautz and his cavalry division were to support Birney until the heights were taken, then push along the Darbytown road toward the capital.

Grant liked the plan and adopted it, partly because it offered a fair hope of capturing Richmond. He also thought that it was certain to draw Confederates north of the river again and thus weaken their hold on the Southside Railroad, one of the last three rail lines serving Lee.

With so much at stake, Butler was determined that his subordinates be fully briefed and that the enemy be kept completely in the dark. On September 28, the day before the attack was scheduled to take place, Butler's headquarters was a scene of endless activity. "Portents of a coming *something* were unmistakable," reported a New York *Times* correspondent. Yet no one knew just what to expect. "In all my experience," wrote the journalist, "I never knew a plan to be kept so profoundly secret."

The corps commanders met with Butler to receive their final instructions — 16 pages of them, providing for every conceivable contingency. But no orders of any kind would be distributed to the men until after nightfall. Butler, riding along the river in the twilight to survey his forces, was delighted to see that they revealed no signs of an impending movement. He watched the construction of the pontoon bridge on which Ord and his troops were to move to the north side of the James. When the bridge had been rigged and muffled with dirt and straw, the quietly tramping thousands began to cross and Butler went back to his headquarters to wait. He sat up most of the night drinking coffee, then rode to Deep Bottom, where a pontoon bridge had been in place since June, and followed Birney's men over. By 4:30 a.m. he was with the black troops assigned to Birney's X Corps, who were waiting to go into the fight.

The firing began at 5 a.m. as Birney's skirmishers pushed back the Confederate pickets north of Deep Bottom and approached the defensive line on New Market Heights. The difficulty in maneuvering through the tangled, swampy countryside so confused the Federal advance that only a single division, under Paine, reached the works; the remainder of the Federal force was blocked on the roads to the rear. And only Colonel Samuel Duncan's brigade, 1,100 men, struck the Confederate earthworks.

At first a dense fog obscured much of the

field. The Confederates, four brigades of Brigadier General John Gregg's division, became aware of the attack only when they heard what Private Joseph B. Polley of the 4th Texas described later as "a roar that sounded like the bellowing of ten thousand wild bulls." Before they could see the approaching Federals, a few excited defenders were jumping on top of the parapets and, as one of them recalled, "shooting at shadows."

Birney found the enemy resistance stiffer than he had expected. Most of the Confederates held their fire until the Federals had splashed across a creek and were struggling through the abatis. The first volley staggered the attackers. "It was a perfectly terrible encounter," remembered Colonel John Ames of the 6th U.S. Colored Troops. "We were all cut to pieces." Birney ordered a second assault, sending Colonel Alonzo Draper's brigade against the earthworks. Draper's men bravely withstood the fire of Colonel Frederick Bass's Texas Brigade for a full 30 minutes. When the shooting slackened, the Federal troops rushed over the parapets. The Confederates were gone.

The 1,800 defenders had realized that they would be overrun if they were to remain. Moreover, they had received word that they were needed to help repel a strong Federal attack on Fort Harrison. With the morning still young, they abandoned New Market Heights to the Federals.

Ord, meanwhile, had pushed his large force briskly up the Varina road just after daylight, driving in the Confederate pickets and pressing to within a mile of Fort Harrison. There the Federals formed a line of battle—and faced a dismaying prospect. They would have to advance across a mile of cleared, rising ground swept by the enemy's

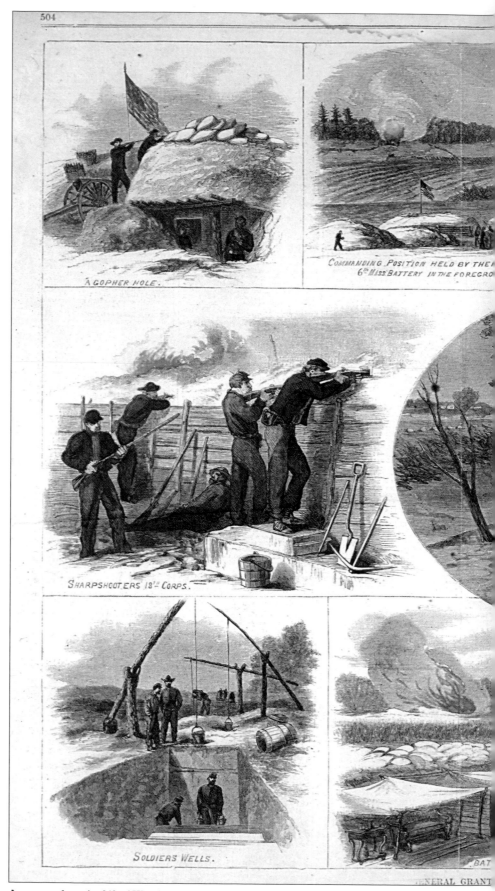

A montage by artist Alfred Waud, sketched at Petersburg during the siege, alternates scenes of Federal

T OF GEN. WARREN.

OFFICERS QUARTERS ON THE FRONT

AIMING A MORTAR IN JACKSONS C⊤ BATTERY.

S CORPS BEHIND THE RIFLE PITS

RTARS AND LIGHT TWELVES 1 ST C⊤ HEAVY ARTILLERY. L⊤ JACKSON. 18 TH CORPS.

MAKING PARALLELS.

IN THE TRENCHES BEFORE PETERSBURG.—SKETCHED BY A. R. WAUD.—[SEE PAGE 502.]

sharpshooters and artillery in action with glimpses of the elaborate measures Grant's men undertook to secure water, shade, and shelter from enemy fire.

guns and muskets. Then they must assault a solid hilltop fort anchored in the entrenchments enclosing Chaffin's Bluff.

Inside these impressive works, however, was a less than impressive garrison: roughly 800 inexperienced, unreliable and badly posted men of the heavy artillery. When they caught sight of the thousands of Federals filing into line of battle, the defenders sprang to their cannon, discovering too late that only four of the seven large-caliber pieces were in working order.

General Ord — who in his long Regular Army career had never before led a major operation — hesitated. The commander of his 1st Division, Brigadier General George S. Stannard, pleaded with Ord to allow him to send his men against the fort, even though the 2nd Division was not yet in supporting position. Confederate reinforcements would be on the way, Stannard argued, and the attack had to be made immediately.

Ord finally assented, and Stannard's three brigades moved forward. The fort's few working guns and the batteries nearby on the Confederate line banged away, firing high and drawing derisive jeers from the advancing Federals. Stannard's men tramped steadily as if on parade, his brigade commanders holding down the pace — even after the enemy guns got the range and began exacting heavy casualties — to avoid exhausting the men with a mile-long dash.

As the Federals drew closer, the Confederates discovered a serious flaw in the defensive works. They could not depress their guns enough to cover the base of the hill that Fort Harrison crowned. The entire Federal division found a refuge here to pause and brace itself for the final assault up the steep slope to the enemy fortifications. While their

troops prepared for the last advance, Ord and Stannard could see General Gregg's Confederate troops rushing westward along the New Market road toward the fort.

In one disorganized mass, the Federal division surged up the hill and into the enemy works. As the howling bluecoats clambered up the earthen ramparts — some on ladders they had improvised by jamming bayonets into the embankment and stepping on the rifle barrels — the poorly disciplined defending force began to fall apart. The reserve units fired their volleys too early, then panicked and ran, leaving the few veteran companies hopelessly outnumbered. These troops had no choice but to withdraw as well. "I gave the order to get out in the best manner possible," recalled Major James B. Moore of the 17th Georgia. "Private A. P. McCord was on top of the traverse embankment firing right down into the midst of the enemy not more than fifteen feet distant. He remained in this perilous position until the bluecoats became as thick within the works as blackbirds upon a millet stack."

Thus by 7 a.m. the New Market road line had been rolled up, and the Federals were in possession of Fort Harrison. Like Burnside at Petersburg two months earlier, Butler had a priceless opportunity: a shattered enemy line, a vital objective close at hand and an overwhelming superiority of numbers. But as Burnside had demonstrated, all these advantages would mean nothing if Butler could not retain tight control over his forces, concentrate them and keep them moving.

This was not going to be easy. Stannard's 1st Division had paid a heavy price for its success at Fort Harrison: Every one of its brigade commanders, four of its regimental commanders and 18 percent of its men were

Among the Federal units entrenched near Petersburg was Company D of the 149th Pennsylvania — some of whose members sported white bucktails on their caps as emblems of marksmanship. In September, however, the company was doing more digging than shooting. "The spade is a very useful weapon," one Union officer observed, "but we have a little too much of it."

casualties. Discipline, too, had become a casualty, even before the final charge. And once the Federals were inside the walls, the exhilaration of victory delayed the restoration of order. An hour passed before any move was made farther into the entrenched Confederate positions. When it came, that movement was slow and tentative.

General Ord desperately needed the fresh units of his 2nd Division to bolster the 1st and to take up the drive inside the Confederate fortifications. But the 2nd Division, uncertainly led by Brigadier General Charles A. Heckman, had meandered far to the right. It had become tangled in some swampy woods and was heading up the Varina road for a frontal attack on the Confederate exterior

line northeast of Fort Harrison, too far away to be a support to or be supported by Stannard's 1st Division.

Frantic to sustain his momentum and facing growing resistance to his right, Ord decided to thrust toward the river, along the trenches to his left. This line, with its two salients, was defended by fewer than 200 Confederates; but Ord was able to pull together only a small attacking force, composed of officers and a few men from Colonel Michael T. Donohoe's battalion of skirmishers. Hoping to inspire them, Ord led the attack personally.

To the south of Fort Harrison, the Confederate gunners of Captain Cornelius T. Allen's Lunenburg Heavy Artillery had kept

up a steady fire on the Federals occupying the works. Now, flanked by Ord's attackers, these Virginia artillerymen abandoned their battery and withdrew down the line of earthworks toward the river. As they retreated, other units joined them, and when they reached a strong point called Fort Hoke, Allen made his stand. Grabbing smoothbore muskets stored in the fort, the artillerymen and reserves managed to stop Ord's attack party cold. Ord himself suffered a painful leg wound that disabled him.

Allen's beleaguered gunners received help from an unexpected source. The *Fredericksburg* and the *Richmond*, two powerful Confederate ironclads, had steamed up the James with an escort of several smaller gunboats and had opened fire on the Federals. The naval gunfire was inaccurate and sporadic, but Ord's Federals were badly shaken by the huge shells crashing near them.

Thus, at a time when everything depended on movement, the Federals were stalled; just when they most needed strong leadership, they had lost their corps commander. Ord reluctantly went to the rear in an ambulance, turning command over to his senior subordinate — who, as fate would have it, was the undistinguished General Heckman. Largely by default, Heckman's division had managed to take a section of the Confederate exterior line northeast of Fort Harrison. But he failed to recognize the possibility of assaulting the enemy lines from the flank and rear. Instead of bringing the 2nd Division into the entrenched camp and attacking the Confederates from behind, Heckman repeatedly ordered his men to make frontal attacks on the strongly held intermediate line.

These thrusts, just outside the northeast corner of the entrenched camp, were made by individual brigades advancing unsup-

The Federal troops ordered to attack Fort Harrison on the morning of September 29 faced this forbidding prospect — a parapet with enclosed gun positions, fronted by a row of sharpened stakes to entangle charging infantry. Such defenses took their toll: The Union division leading the assault suffered 92 men killed and 502 wounded before the day was out.

ported into brutal enfilading fire. For two hours Heckman's exhausted men and their confused officers stumbled forward time and again and were shot down in droves. By 10 a.m. the survivors were fought out, the assaults had stopped and a lull was spreading over the field.

About this time General Grant arrived in the area, not to exercise any control over the fighting — as usual, he was leaving that to his subordinates — but simply to assess the situation for himself. When Grant appeared at New Market Heights to talk with Butler and Birney, the troops of X Corps cheered him, as one New Yorker remembered it, "till they fairly raised the old fellow, cigar and all, from his saddle."

Grant then rode over to Fort Harrison. Although he could not perceive it, Richmond, eight miles to the north, was in an unprecedented state of alarm. It was not the fall of Fort Harrison that frightened the citizens, for they had not yet learned of it; they were transfixed by the roar of artillery a mere two miles east of the city: General Kautz and his 2,200 Federal cavalrymen were almost at the gates of Richmond, attacking a section of the intermediate line held by a small but stubborn force of Confederate artillery.

As ordered, Kautz had headed north as soon as Birney's corps had taken New Market Heights. In a short time, his troopers reached the Darbytown road, and at 10 a.m. they moved forward to make the attack. But the little band of defenders, 100 men of Major James Hensley's 10th Virginia Heavy Artillery Battalion, opened fire with their half-dozen or so cannon and quickly discouraged Kautz. He led his men back into the safety of the woods and stayed there, apparently losing all sense of urgency. It took him three

hours to move his command a mile north, to the Charles City road, and attack again. By that time, a somewhat stronger enemy force was ready to meet him.

Upon hearing the sounds of Kautz's attack and the thunderous defense so close at hand, officials in Richmond had dragooned convicts and convalescents, and Major General James L. Kemper had called out the 4,500 men and boys of his Local Defense Force. Many of these last-ditch reinforcements had reached the Charles City road by the time Kautz got there at 1:30 p.m., and the faint-hearted Union commander again retreated at the first sign of opposition. Then for four hours he stayed put, unable to decide what to do, until slowly and gingerly he began to move northward — away from Richmond.

General Grant, visiting Fort Harrison shortly after Kautz's initial attack, apparently took at face value the achievement of the operation's first objectives and did not detect any signs of impending disaster. He simply scrawled a message to Birney saying that XVIII Corps was ready to advance on Richmond and that Birney's X Corps should do likewise. Then the general in chief returned to Deep Bottom to await developments.

On the Confederate side of the lines, these developments were now coming fast. The ailing Lieutenant General Richard S. Ewell, whom Lee had gently removed from corps command and put in charge of the defenses of Richmond, rose to the occasion with all of his former ferocity. Taking personal charge of the threatened encampment at Chaffin's Bluff, the one-legged Ewell had thrown a line diagonally across its wooded interior, from the embattled redans on the river northeastward to Fort Johnson on the opposite corner. The line was little more than a façade, manned by badly shaken heavy artillerymen now forced to fight as infantry and by Major Alexander W. Starke's battalion of light artillery. Ewell, however, was a gambler; he rode up and down the line, pushing skirmishers to the edge of the woods facing the Federals. "I remember very distinctly how he looked," recalled one of his soldiers, "mounted on an old gray horse, as mad as he could be, shouting to the men and seeming to be everywhere at once." The ruse worked. No Federals advanced from Fort Harrison.

As serious as the situation was at Chaffin's Bluff, General Lee also had to worry about what the Federals were doing south of the river. The previous day they had shown signs of concentrating on the left of their lines below Petersburg — a deliberate deception — and since dawn on the 29th there had been further ominous indications of movement there.

Throughout the morning Lee waited, until he could be certain about his enemy's intentions. Finally, at midday, he decided that the thrust north of the river was the real peril, and he moved decisively. He ordered substantial reinforcements to march north toward the embattled Confederate position, and in early afternoon he, too, headed for Chaffin's Bluff.

By this time General Birney and the Federal X Corps were struggling northeast along the New Market road, supposedly to join XVIII Corps in the drive toward Richmond. Birney's 2nd Division, under Brigadier General Robert S. Foster, took the lead. Exhausted by their long night march and forced to fight every step that morning against persistent rearguard actions, Foster's men were literally dropping out by the hundreds. When the rapidly weakening force approached the intersection of the New Market and Varina roads, Foster found, instead of an inviting gap in the Confederate defenses, the bristling works of the intermediate line.

Just to the southwest of the intersection loomed the squat expanse of Fort Gilmer, a salient only slightly less imposing than Fort Harrison. It, too, was poorly designed and undermanned, and again the Federals threw against it a vastly superior force. But Birney's attack had none of the punch that had been delivered against Fort Harrison.

After a considerable delay, Birney wheeled his 2nd Division to attack southward, but the inexperienced General Foster deployed his men in a thin line of battle with no reserves. Meanwhile, Brigadier General William Birney, older brother of the X Corps commander, prepared his brigade of black troops for a simultaneous attack westward, against the salient's other wall.

Foster's men struggled forward through three brush-tangled ravines, under intensifying artillery fire. "Death fairly reveled in that third ravine," a survivor recalled. "Shells hissed and exploded about our ears incessantly, and crushed heads and mangled bodies thickly strewed our pathway."

Confederate reinforcements — including Colonel Bass with some of the Texans who had lost their race to Fort Harrison — were streaming into the works. They brought their rifles to bear as the Federals emerged from the last ravine and charged across a cornfield. The attackers could manage only a few steps into the furious hail of bullets and canister. Leaving scores of dead and wounded comrades behind, they fled back into the deadly ravine.

General Paine's entire division was in reserve behind Foster's men, but despite the

As a shell bursts overhead, General Grant calmly writes a dispatch from Fort Harrison, captured a few hours earlier by Federal troops. "Those standing about instinctively ducked their heads," wrote Horace Porter, Grant's aide, "but he paid no attention to the occurrence, and did not pause in his writing, or even look up.

"a whirlwind seemed to rush across our front. The line disappeared as though an earthquake had swallowed it."

It was impossible to go forward, unthinkable to remain; Foster ordered retreat, leaving 400 of his men and 100 men of the black regiment dead or wounded on the field. In all, the 2nd Division had lost 35 percent of its men as casualties, and for the time being, it was finished as a fighting force.

About 2:30 p.m., the first of the Confederate reinforcements from Petersburg—a brigade from General Charles Field's division led by Colonel Pinckney D. Bowles—arrived at Fort Gilmer. With these troops came their corps commander, Lieutenant General Richard Anderson, and General Lee.

Only now did William Birney get his Federal troops in position to begin the attack on the western wall that should have coincided with Foster's. The Confederates, heartened by their repulse of the 2nd Division and by the arrival of fresh troops, turned all their firepower on Birney's advancing brigade.

This attack was even more piecemeal than Foster's had been. The men were sent forward a regiment at a time into a storm of bullets and artillery fire that consumed them at a ghastly rate. The 9th U.S. Colored Troops under Captain Edward Babcock got halfway to the fort before being driven back into the woods to their rear. But four companies of Colonel James Shaw's 7th U.S. Colored Troops—men recruited in Maryland—deployed as skirmishers and rushed the fort alone. The 189 men advanced under galling fire and piled through the abatis and into the ditch at the base of the fort. Though half of them already were casualties, the rest tried valiantly to scale the walls. The defenders shot every man who raised his head over

gravity of the moment, David Birney sent only one of Paine's regiments, the 5th U.S. Colored Troops, to reinforce Foster so that he could regroup and attack again. A Federal who made the second charge recalled, "The leaves of corn, cut by flying shot, floated before our eyes continually, and fell to the earth in showers." The assault force made it to within 40 paces of the works, he wrote, when

the parapet and dropped short-fused howitzer shells into the ditch. A mere handful of survivors were taken prisoner; only one man returned to the Federal lines.

The Federal drive had been stopped, and the troops could not stay where they were. Confederate reinforcements now pouring over the Chaffin's Bluff bridge posed a serious threat to the Federal left and rear. The Federals saw this danger early in the afternoon, and General Stannard ordered a defensive line prepared. In late afternoon David Birney drew X Corps back along the New Mar-

ket road to make a junction with the XVIII Corps right, and Heckman refused his left by forming a new line from Fort Harrison back to the river. The Federals began to fortify their positions as best they could, throwing up a wall across the open end of Fort Harrison, reversing some old Confederate works, digging new trenches where they had to and preparing for the counterattack they knew would come in the morning.

The Federal high command was worried about what had become of Kautz. During the afternoon and evening of the 29th, his cavalry had groped its way northward almost

Advancing in three lines of battle on September 30, Confederates bent on retaking Fort Harrison come up against a compact skirmish line of Federals (*foreground*) firing from behind a rail fence. Those attackers who pushed past the skirmishers to within range of the fort faced a more galling reception — a concentrated volley whose din one South Carolinian likened to "the magnified roar of a thousand kettle drums."

to the Chickahominy River. There, at midnight, Kautz attempted a feeble attack on the Confederate intermediate line where it bent to the west, and after a confusing and ineffective round of firing at one another as much as at the enemy, the Federals mounted up again and rode back to the south. At 7:30 in the morning Kautz's riders rejoined X Corps on the Federal right.

All night long, while the Federal infantry had been digging, Confederate reinforcements had been tramping across the bridge to Chaffin's Bluff. They were veterans, the infantry divisions of Field and Hoke, supported by E. Porter Alexander's battalion of seven field batteries, numbering 30 guns. By morning nearly 12,000 men had joined the battered 4,000 who held the remnant of the entrenched camp and the intermediate line. For all the desperate fighting of the day before, Confederate casualties had been light, around 400 men; Butler's Army of the James had lost 3,000. The 21,000 Federals who remained, with their poor leadership and uncertain fighting qualities, had little advantage over the 16,000 Confederates who were on the field by the morning of September 30.

The Federals were utterly worn out after 36 hours of marching, fighting and digging. For that reason and also because Grant was preparing to deliver another blow south of the James that day, Butler went on the defensive. He placed his chief engineer, Major General Godfrey Weitzel, in command of Ord's XVIII Corps and concentrated his forces in the middle of the Federal line, between Fort Harrison on the south and the New Market road to the north.

The attack did not come in the morning — Lee was not ready until midafternoon — but when it came, it looked awesome. Lee had given the task of leading the assault to General Richard Anderson, who devised a sledgehammer blow against Fort Harrison.

Anderson massed Hoke's five brigades in the interior of the entrenched camp, concealed in a ravine, and aimed them straight east at Fort Harrison. But before they advanced, Field's group of three brigades was to swing down from the north, along the camp wall. They were to go as far as a depression immediately in front of the earthworks just erected by the Federals in the fort's open rear and wait there until Hoke's brigades came up. Then all 9,000 Confederates would charge the makeshift defensive position, which was held by about 2,000 Federals.

It was a bold plan, just the kind Lee's army had executed flawlessly in many battles. But this was not the old Army of Northern Virginia, as soon became apparent.

Field's lead brigade, advancing to the southeast along the camp wall, was commanded by Brigadier General George T. (Tige) Anderson. To Anderson's horror, once he got his Georgians moving, he could not get them to stop at the appointed place; they ran on heedlessly, attacking the fortifications without support and without hope of success. While Lee and Richard Anderson looked on in frustration, Tige Anderson's brigade was shattered by the Federals.

The initial loss of control threw the entire attack into disorder. Brigadier General John Bratton's South Carolina brigade struggled through Anderson's fleeing Georgians to attack, only to meet a similar fate. Not until Colonel Bowles's Alabamians, the last of Field's three brigades, had been repulsed did the first two of Hoke's brigades come into action; when they did, a Federal soldier recalled, "We mowed them down like grass."

Lee watched in anguish as more than 1,200 troops were needlessly shot down. He took a hand in re-forming the shaken survivors of the attack, one witness reporting later that the commanding general's face was "as long as a gun barrel." Federal possession of Fort Harrison, threatening as it was to Chaffin's Bluff and the intermediate line, was intolerable to Lee. But for the moment, as General Bratton put it, the task of recapturing the fort was "too much for human valor." Besides, there was fresh trouble simmering, south of the James.

That morning, four Federal divisions of infantry and one of cavalry had begun to move around the overextended Confederate line below Petersburg. They were headed for the Southside Railroad, one of the rail lines still serving the city.

Grant, although intrigued by the possibility of a windfall victory north of the river, regarded Butler's operations there as secondary to the main business of severing railroads. The moment Lee weakened his Petersburg forces to deal with Butler, Grant unleashed General Warren to the south.

With two divisions of V Corps, Warren was to strike westward from the Federal left at Globe Tavern. He was to turn the Confederate right — a redoubt about a mile away, near Poplar Springs Church — then drive north to the Boydton Plank Road, a major artery leading into Petersburg from the southwest. From there the Southside Railroad would be within easy reach. Following Warren to his left were General Parke with two IX Corps divisions and General David Gregg with his cavalry.

Warren's leading division came upon the Confederate redoubt and unfinished works, defended by Colonel Joel Griffin's independent brigade of cavalry and Captain Edward Graham's Petersburg Battery. They were located a few hundred yards beyond Poplar Springs Church on a farm owned by a man named Peeble. The Federals took their time, driving in Colonel Griffin's skirmishers and working their way up a wooded ravine toward the fort. Despite the fire of Graham's guns, Warren was able to concentrate Brigadier General Charles Griffin's division a mere 100 yards from the redoubt under cover of the woods. Some of the Federals, chafing under the sporadic cannon fire, attacked before the order was given. At this, the entire line rushed forward in broken formation and swept cheering into the fort. The Confederates took to their heels, barely managing to save two of their three guns.

By now, General Parke's IX Corps had passed Warren on the left, heading northwest toward the Boydton Plank Road. But Parke's command was moving lethargically, and on reaching a wooded area a short distance away, it halted. "Parke seemed unable to determine what to do," recalled Colonel Charles Wainwright.

The Confederate defense of Petersburg at this hour was the responsibility of Lieutenant General A. P. Hill — General Beauregard had been assigned to new duties farther south. Hill wasted no time in sending the divisions of Major Generals Heth and Wilcox out to meet the new threat on their right.

They were there when Warren impatiently rode out to join the indecisive Parke. The Federal commanders were confronted by a line of earthworks to the north, and while they deliberated, Confederate soldiers were digging frantically to extend that line. Wain-

In a painting by Confederate veteran William Sheppard, a circle of Petersburg's defenders study a newspaper outside a bombproof that the men have labeled "Spottswood Hotel," after one of Richmond's finest hostelries. The news in September 1864 of Confederate defeats in Georgia and the Shenandoah Valley did nothing to hearten the men in the trenches.

wright recorded in his diary that a mile to the west could be seen "a line of red dirt thrown up, and men still working." These defenses were not yet fully manned, but for all his urging, Warren could not get Parke moving.

Not until late afternoon did Parke order a division forward to the attack. Before the Federals reached the enemy trenches, however, they met an advancing skirmish line; the Confederates were attacking them.

The Federal division commander, Brigadier General Robert B. Potter, continued his assault. Potter thought he was going to be supported on the right by one of Warren's divisions. But no such arrangement had been made, and Potter was soon outflanked by a sweeping attack by two of Wilcox's bri-

gades and driven back. At the sight of this repulse, the hapless IX Corps came apart again, stampeding for the rear; it lost 480 men killed and wounded, and a staggering 1,300 were taken prisoner.

Parke managed to stop the disgraceful rout with his reserve division, which was anchored on Warren's firm position at the Peeble farm. The Confederates tried hard to break through. The 1st and the 14th South Carolina pressed close to the Federal line but could not stand in the face of fire from Warren's 34 guns. When Major General James J. Archer's brigade swept down the Church road to attack the Federal right, General Griffin ordered Captain Charles E. Minks to place his 1st New York Artillery in front of

With brandished sword, Colonel Norval Welch of the 16th Michigan leaps into the Confederate works at the Peeble farm on September 30, drawing the fire of an enemy marksman (*left*). Welch did not live to savor the triumphant charge of his regiment, part of Warren's V Corps. A subordinate recalled Welch standing on the barricade just before he died, "cheering and encouraging the men of the entire brigade to come forward."

the infantry. "My God, General," cried the astonished Captain, "do you mean for me to put my guns out on the skirmish line?"

"Yes," replied Griffin. "Rush them in there; artillery is not better than infantry, put them in line and let them fight together."

The guns stopped the Confederate drive, and the next day, reinforced by another division, IX Corps advanced again. The Federals' intent was not to attack the Confederate defenses but to establish a forward line of their own. The men immediately began to fortify this new position with trenches and redoubts, connecting it with Globe Tavern, a mile to the east.

This was another mile that Lee had to defend, and his costs were approaching the un-

bearable. A few days after the loss of Fort Harrison he had informed the Confederate Secretary of War, James A. Seddon, that things could not long continue in this way. While Grant extended his lines and increased his numbers, Lee wrote, the Army of Northern Virginia could "only meet his corps, increased by recent recruits, with a division, reduced by long and arduous service."

Deeply depressed, Lee began to speak openly for the first time of the possibility of losing Richmond. He needed time to find more men, more food, more ammunition and more horses. His hope now was to hang on until cold, wet weather put a temporary end to Grant's incessant attacks. "We may be able, with the blessing of God, to keep the enemy in check until the beginning of winter," he wrote. "If we fail to do this the result may be calamitous."

But Lee was never content simply to defend, and even in this crisis he was looking for an opportunity to attack. He was also determined to repair the damage done to the defenses of Richmond. In early October he ordered an assault down the New Market and Darbytown roads, where Kautz's Federal cavalry, now reduced to 1,700 men, held the former exterior line of entrenchments. Lee hoped to drive Kautz from his position, thus turning the Federal right, and then envelop the enemy line as far toward the James as he could. On October 6 he moved Field's and Hoke's divisions into position to challenge Kautz.

At first light on October 7, two of Hoke's brigades quietly worked their way through their old fortifications north of the Darbytown road and hit Kautz's right flank. At the same time, two of Field's brigades attacked Kautz's front. When Brigadier General

Martin W. Gary's Confederate cavalry brigade attacked their rear, the Federal horsemen fell back in confusion, losing all eight of their guns. They retreated to the south, reforming behind the trenches held by Brigadier General Alfred H. Terry's more stalwart X Corps division.

Pressing his advantage, Lee ordered an assault on Terry's position by Field's and Hoke's full divisions. But at 10 a.m., when Lee asked one of his aides if the two divisions were ready to charge, the answer was: "None but the Texas Brigade, General." Sadly, but with pride, Lee replied, "The Texas Brigade is always ready."

Field's division soon went forward — the Texans leading the way — only to run up against a jumble of trees felled on the path. As the men struggled to pass through this barrier, the line of assault disintegrated into scattered groups, losing coordination and coming under heavy fire from the enemy. "There was no staying in line, and could be none," Private Joseph B. Polley wrote later. "It was each one for himself."

Worse, for reasons never adequately explained, Hoke did not join in the attack. Field's men were alone in the face of a roused foe. They fought on for a time, but to no avail. During the struggle, the division's commander, General John Gregg, fell dead with a bullet through his neck. Having lost 1,350 men, Lee gave up hope of restoring the exterior line. Realistically he turned his attention instead to building new fortifications closer to Richmond.

Federal casualties were minimal in this latest fighting, and the Confederates had not been able to drive the Union troops from the positions they had gained north of the James. But the Federals seemed unable to get any closer to Richmond. Grant, neither flustered nor impatient, simply stayed with his plan to cut at Lee's railroad life lines by pushing left, then right, stretching the Confederate army to its limits of manpower.

On the gloomy morning of October 27, in a cold rain presaging the winter weather that would soon bring campaigning to a standstill, the Army of the Potomac moved out again on its left. Its objective, once more, was the Southside Railroad.

General Parke was to take part of IX Corps two miles to the west of Poplar Springs Church and confront the extreme Confederate right where the earthworks ran to a winding little stream called Hatcher's Run. The Federals believed these fortifications to be incomplete and lightly manned. If Parke could surprise the enemy and break through the line, he was to continue his drive north toward the railroad four miles away. Warren, with most of V Corps, would support Parke on the left, following the stream northwest. If Parke could not advance, Warren would try to turn the enemy flank. Meanwhile, Hancock with two of his divisions, screened by David Gregg's cavalry division on the left, would cross Hatcher's Run, then turn northwest and head for the railroad. Thus the entire Federal force of 40,000 infantry, 3,000 cavalry and their artillery would be on the move — Hancock to the west of Hatcher's Run, Warren and Parke to the east. They were marching against little more than half their number.

The Federals began slogging through the drizzle and mud long before daylight. Parke determined that the enemy line east of the stream was too strong to attack and, as ordered to do in that eventuality, he contented himself with making threatening maneuvers. Warren moved into position on the IX Corps left, skirmishing and looking for an advantage. Hancock moved his two divisions out vigorously, brushing aside enemy pickets and reaching the Boydton Plank Road at midday. He was now more than a mile ahead of V Corps to his right.

The gap between Hancock and Warren was of particular concern to General Meade, who had come onto the field accompanied by Grant. He ordered Hancock to wait and to extend his right while Warren closed up.

Warren sent Brigadier General Samuel W. Crawford's division across Hatcher's Run to move forward and form a junction with Hancock. But between the two forces was a mile of dense, trackless woods. The stream wound through this thicket so tortuously that Crawford's men began getting lost in great numbers as they tried to follow it. Crawford ordered the men to halt, re-form and get their bearings.

Once again in this devilish campaign,

Hancock and II Corps were on their own. The afternoon was wearing on, and the high command decided it was too late in the day to continue the advance toward the Southside Railroad. Hancock received instructions to hold his position — on the Boydton Plank Road, where it crossed Hatcher's Run — until nightfall, then withdraw.

But the Confederates had no intention of letting Hancock stay there unmolested. While elements of Wade Hampton's cavalry had fought ferociously to delay the potentially disastrous Federal flanking movement, General A. P. Hill had sent Heth's division racing down the Boydton Plank Road to strike Hancock's center, which by that time was aligned across the road and along Hatcher's Run. Hampton then started north to flank the Federal left, and Mahone's division swung to the south, into the thick woods, to emerge on Hancock's right rear.

Easily picking their way through the thickets that had stopped the Federal V Corps, Mahone's Confederates slammed into Colonel Byron R. Pierce's brigade, which was serving as the rear guard for the division commanded by Brigadier General Thomas Egan. At the time, around four in the afternoon, Egan was about to lead a thrust across Hatcher's Run on the Boydton Plank Road bridge. Attacked from behind, Egan had to change front and try to fight his way back toward the main body.

"I shall never forget that day or that battle," wrote another of Egan's brigade commanders, Colonel Robert McAllister. "Surrounded on all sides, cut off from the balance of our corps, our fate seemed to be sealed without a hope of escape." But these Federals were commanded by Hancock, not by Burnside or Butler. Coolly and quickly re-forming his men and redeploying his guns, Hancock threw a solid line of resistance along the plank road to face Mahone's charge while Egan, although running out of ammunition, mounted a countercharge that took Mahone in flank. The Confederate attack was not only stopped, it was shattered and driven back into the woods in confusion.

Moments later five brigades of Hampton's cavalry charged Hancock's left and rear, but they encountered the formidable Gregg. With timely support from Hancock's infantry, Gregg's riders held their ground.

In this encounter Wade Hampton suffered more than defeat. While his men fought dismounted, the courtly South Carolina planter and his staff officers rode in the advance. One of his aides was his son and namesake, Lieutenant Wade Hampton; his other son, Preston, also a lieutenant, fought nearby with his own men.

During the charge, Preston fell with a bullet in the groin. As soon as the line passed him, his brother, Wade, rushed to his side, dismounted and was himself shot in the back. As he fell, their horrified father galloped over to them.

Young Wade was not badly hurt and was able to get up. But General Hampton, who had himself been wounded at Bull Run, at Seven Pines and at Gettysburg, had seen enough dying men to recognize the look on Preston's face. Weeping in anguish, the general accompanied Preston to the rear of the lines. When a surgeon came over to inspect the wound, the general waved him away with a curt "Too late, doctor." Then, after taking one more look at the pale and stricken face of his son, General Hampton turned away and rode toward the guns.

The shooting continued until well after

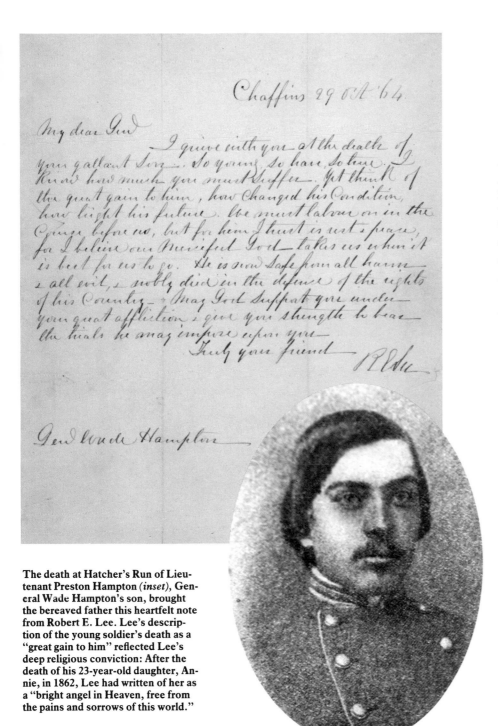

Chaffins 29 Oct '64.

My dear Genl

I grieve with you at the death of your gallant Son... So young, so brave, so true. I know how much you must suffer... Yet think of the great gain to him, how changed his Condition, how bright his future... We must labour on in the Course before us, but for him I trust is rest & peace, for I believe our Merciful God... takes us when it is best for us to go... He is now safe from all harm & all evil, & nobly died in the defence of the rights of his Country... May God support you under your great affliction & give you strength to bear the trials he may impose upon you—

Truly your friend — R E Lee

Genl Wade Hampton

The death at Hatcher's Run of Lieutenant Preston Hampton *(inset)*, General Wade Hampton's son, brought the bereaved father this heartfelt note from Robert E. Lee. Lee's description of the young soldier's death as a "great gain to him" reflected Lee's deep religious conviction: After the death of his 23-year-old daughter, Annie, in 1862, Lee had written of her as a "bright angel in Heaven, free from the pains and sorrows of this world."

that he would "work this thing out all right yet." But the solution would have to wait. Now, as happened every year in Virginia, the cold autumn rains came more and more frequently. Often the downpours lasted for days and made the roads impassable to wagons and artillery. With the increasing threat that any movement might be caught by such weather and bog down, Grant was forced to suspend his constant hammering at the 35-mile-long Confederate line. In a sense, Lee had won a limited victory, for he had held out until winter.

The Federal army's strength, although increased from its August low point, constantly threatened to erode again. In late October Major Theodore S. Bowers of Grant's staff wrote that replacements were "barely sufficient to make up for losses in battle and by expiration of enlistments." He concluded that the government was reluctant to raise more men "until after the election. Everything now hinges on the elections."

The time was at hand for selecting the next President of the United States. In the last days of October there was repeated, throughout the Army of the Potomac and the other farflung armies of the Union, an unprecedented scene: soldiers in the midst of a protracted civil war voting, in an orderly manner, on whether to retain in power their commander in chief. Their ballots were collected and sent to their home states so that the votes could be counted on the official election day, November 8.

The voters had to choose between a popular former army commander who promised peace — George McClellan — and a controversial, much-misunderstood country lawyer, often portrayed as a bumbler, who vowed to fight the War to its conclusion. By a

dark, and while the Confederates could not force Hancock from his position, neither could he get past them to the Southside Railroad. During the night, II Corps withdrew to its original lines. It had suffered 1,482 casualties and had made little headway.

Still Grant gave no sign of being perturbed. The night after the battle had ended at Hatcher's Run, he wrote to his wife, Julia,

large majority, soldiers and civilians alike voted for Abraham Lincoln.

General Grant sent to Washington a telegram of congratulation, not just for the victory but for the way in which it was achieved: "The election having passed off quietly, no bloodshed or riot throughout the land, is a victory worth more to the country than a battle won." Hours later, Grant sent another telegram — a portent of what the victory would mean — "All the troops now in the North will be hurried to the field."

Grant was at last unshackled from the constraints of politics that had stayed his hand in innumerable ways since he had taken command. He had fought resolutely and with single-mindedness; now he became more willing to take chances and less tolerant of lackluster performance.

On November 15, Grant allowed General Sherman to take the extraordinary risk of severing his line of communications to Atlanta and disappearing with his 60,000-man army in a march toward the sea. And as the year closed, Grant finally freed himself of a subordinate who, until the election was decided, had been untouchable. On Christmas Day, General Butler blundered an attack on Fort Fisher at Wilmington, North Carolina, thus failing to close the last major Confederate seaport. Butler had delayed the operation endlessly while he tinkered with an old ship filled with black powder that he intended to use to blow up Fort Fisher; as it turned out, the ship blew up nothing but itself, and Butler's attack was a fiasco. Grant relieved Butler of command and sent him home to Massachusetts, there to enjoy a long career as Congressman, Governor and eventual candidate for President.

While Sherman more than justified

Grant's gamble by sweeping out of a devastated Georgia to take the port of Savannah, the Army of the Potomac and the Army of Northern Virginia huddled in their trenches and tried to keep warm. To shelter themselves from the snow and rain, the soldiers built sprawling cities of huts made from logs and mud, which they kept heated with fireplaces fashioned from sticks and more mud.

Despite the rudeness of their shelter, the Federals were well fed and well clothed. The Confederates, however, were on the verge of starvation. Hampton's captured herd of beef cattle had not lasted long, and there was little to replace it. North of the James, in a region not so thoroughly despoiled, foraging provided some relief from hunger. But for Confederates south of the river, the winter was a long season of deprivation. Sometimes the men went a week without meat of any kind. When some rancid beef from Nassau filtered through the Federal blockade, one Confederate speculated, "It would not be incredible for the blockading fleet to allow it to come through in hope of poisoning us."

Despite the Confederates' cold and hunger, the work of siege life had to go on, further debilitating the ill-clad and undernourished men. They dug several mines, none of which they ever exploded; they excavated more and more trenches and built up more fortifications. Sometimes they had to dig through frozen ground; at other times they worked in endless muck. Hundreds of brave men who had faced every danger for nearly four years simply could not take any more, and they deserted.

It was not surprising that, in a time of such travail, a religious revival spread through the Federal and Confederate camps. "The whole army has taken to praying," wrote one Lou-

A Confederate invites enemy fire from atop an embankment at Petersburg as a servant in the trench below strums a banjo in this 1864 painting by Winslow Homer. Though Homer used his imagination to create the scene, such acts were not uncommon. One man in the trenches wondered if those who took such risks were simply seeking a swift dispatch from their ordeal: "It was enough to make men mad and reckless."

isiana artilleryman. There were nightly prayer meetings, and some regiments, exhausted though the men were, found the energy to construct rude chapels.

But the average man changed neither his allegiance nor his religion; he simply endured. "The soldiers cooked, ate and slept, played cards, checkers, cribbage and chess, laughed, talked, jested and joked," recorded Private Polley, "and, strange to say, were not altogether unhappy." When pay arrived — for the Confederates it was four months late in coming — the men spent it with abandon. When the money was gone, they reverted to bartering through the lines, exchanging newspapers, tobacco, peanuts, coffee and bacon. Officers generally were tolerant of this illicit trade, and it was understood that no one was to shoot while the trading took place. "When we weren't killing each other," one Federal remembered, "we were the best of friends."

On the last Thursday of November, proclaimed Thanksgiving Day by President Lincoln, the Federal armies outside Richmond and Petersburg, now 120,000 strong and growing, enjoyed a feast of turkey or chicken, pies and fruit. The 57,000 men of the Army of Northern Virginia, however envious, ceased firing in recognition of the Union holiday.

There was no such celebration for Lee's troops. "We lay in grim repose," wrote Captain James F. J. Caldwell of the 1st South Carolina, "and expected the renewal of the mortal conflict. The conviction everywhere prevailed that we could sustain but one more campaign."

In a photograph of a City Point wharf *(left)*, quartermaster wagons gather to receive supplies from newly arrived ships. The lower left of Edward Henry's painting *(below)* shows a similar scene from a different angle.

The congestion of war that descended on City Point is captured in Edward Henry's painting. Henry selected an offshore site from which to depict a portion of City

A Southern Terminal for Northern Abundance

In mid-June of 1864, as Grant's line of operations shifted south, the Union army established a huge new supply base at the confluence of the James and Appomattox Rivers, transforming the hamlet of City Point, Virginia, almost overnight into one of the world's busiest seaports. Eight wharves were constructed along the riverfront to handle the daily flow of more than 200 ships from the North, and the battered City Point Railroad was repaired and extended to the Union lines at Petersburg, six miles away.

Thousands of soldiers and civilian workers inhabited the town. Among them was an energetic 23-year-old artist named Edward Lamson Henry, trained in Europe, who was attached to the army as a captain's clerk. Henry spent his free time roving about City Point making sketches, which he later refined into the panoramic oil painting below.

Here and on the following pages, a combination of photographs taken in 1864 and details from Henry's painting present an intimate look at the booming camp that seemed to one officer to have "sprung out of the earth as if by magic."

Point's bustling waterfront and the mixture of U.S. Army tents and private homes on the promontory that gave the village its name.

Importing the Sustenance of War

Bales of hay and barrels of salt pork fill the foreground in this detail from Henry's panorama, and in the background a coffin is shipped out.

A work gang uses fresh-cut logs to enlarge a wharf in order to keep pace with City Point's heavy shipping traffic. An average of 75 sailing vessels, 40 steamboats and 100 barges delivered men, munitions and stores each day.

Stevedores unload a cargo ship (below) in a dock scene similar to the one in Henry's painting. Each day almost 600 tons of grain and hay moved through City Point to feed the horses, mules and cattle of the Federal army.

New caissons and limbers for field artillery line a 500-foot dock leading to City Point's ordnance wharf. The wharf had been relocated offshore after a Confederate spy's bomb triggered a munitions explosion that claimed several lives.

163

Horse-drawn steam engines, used for running the machinery in City Point's sawmills and repair shops, await delivery on a dock near the quartermaster warehouses. Such engines also powered the pumps that provided the camp's water supply.

A soldier stands guard over a line of 12-pounder Napoleon guns and limbers recently arrived from arsenals in the North. The guns were later forwarded by train to Union artillery units at Petersburg.

Men of the quartermaster corps face the camera from atop carefully stacked crates and barrels at a depot near City Point. Supplies poured into the camp in quantities that one observer called "not merely profusion, but extravagance."

An "Extravagant" Influx of Men and Machines

Fresh men, horses and guns for the Army of the Potomac arrive at City Point by seagoing steamer in this segment of Henry's painting.

Amenities in a Tent City

Soldiers billeted in tents go about camp life on the bluff overlooking the Appomattox River.

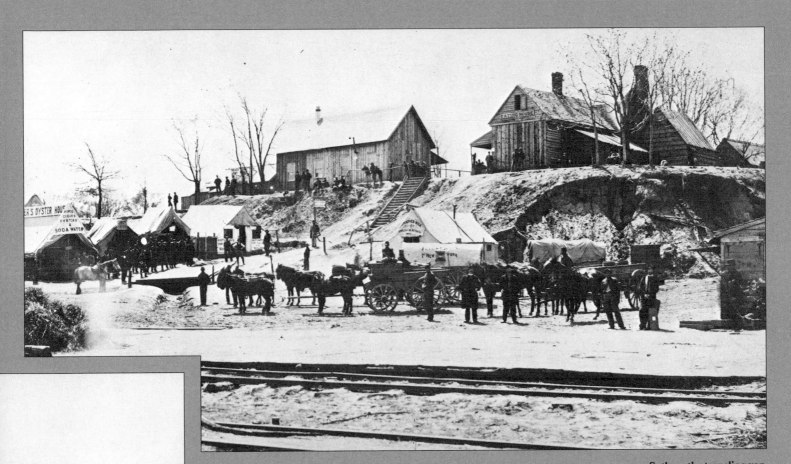

The half-completed army bakery on City Point's bluff eventually produced 123,000 loaves of bread each day. Distribution was so efficient that the loaves were often delivered warm to the troops in camp.

Sutlers, the traveling vendors who followed the army, sold nonration food, drink and other amenities to the soldiers at City Point from this blufftop array of stores and eating houses. The tent at far left offered oysters, a camp favorite.

City Point's crude stockade for military prisoners, shown here under construction, was dreaded by Federal soldiers, who called it the bull pen. One officer said he would have preferred six months' incarceration in a Confederate prison to one month in the bull pen.

Brigadier General Rufus Ingalls (*top center*), chief quartermaster of the Union armies in Virginia, entertains visitors at Appomattox Manor, one of City Point's grandest houses. Grant chose not to use the manor, and other officers grew resentful when the chief quartermaster moved in: "Ingalls is the only one having a house," wrote Colonel Charles Wainwright. "But then, he always took care to be better off than anyone else."

A Contrast in Quarters

Henry painted the area of Grant's quarters with care. Here, the 4th U.S. Infantry band plays at Appomattox Manor as Grant sits at left center.

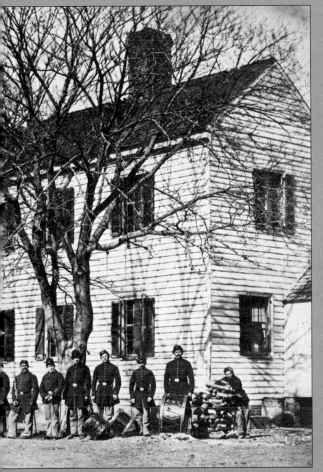

The 4th U.S. Infantry band, arrayed at left in front of the Porter house, serenaded Grant each night he was at City Point, in the mistaken belief that the general enjoyed music. The performances ceased when the tone-deaf Grant remarked, "I've noticed that band always begins its noise just about the time I am sitting down to dinner and want to talk."

General Grant received his visiting wife, Julia, and their son Jesse in this humble planked cabin on the lawn of Appomattox Manor. After spending several months in a tent, Grant moved into the two-room cabin when it became clear that the Petersburg siege would last through the winter.

A Rail Link to the Front

The 59,000-pound locomotive General Dix is photographed arriving at City Point by barge. The Union routinely shipped its trains to City Point this way; one fleet of 90 steamers, tugs and barges delivered two dozen engines and 275 boxcars.

Henry's painting shows the railroad winding along the base of the bluff at City Point. At far right, mounted on a flatcar, is the 8.5-ton mortar called the Dictator.

Wood-burning locomotives run on rails newly laid by the U.S. Military Railroads Construction Corps. The tracks were functional, but rough; one officer compared the bumpy progress of a train moving along them to "a fly crawling on a corrugated washboard."

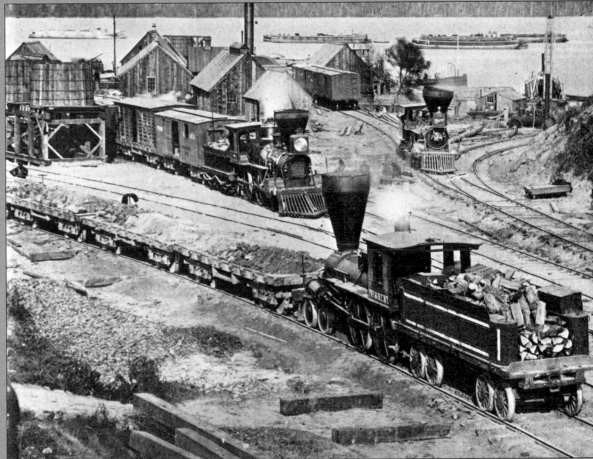

A stretch of riverbank at City Point was cleared and leveled by the Railroads Construction Corps to make room for this enginehouse and yard. The 2,000-man corps also restored the existing City Point Railroad and laid 21 miles of new track.

ACKNOWLEDGMENTS

The editors wish to thank the following individuals and institutions for their valuable assistance in the preparation of this volume:

Massachusetts: Andover — Nicki Thiras, The Addison Gallery of American Art.

Pennsylvania: Carlisle Barracks — Randy W. Hackenburg,

Michael J. Winey, United States Army Military History Institute. Philadelphia — Michael Cavanaugh, Civil War Book Exchange.

Virginia: Petersburg — James H. Bailey, Petersburg Museums; James Blankenship, Chris Calkins, National Park Service, U.S. Department of the Interior; Francis Gilliam; Sergei

Troubetzkoy, The Siege Museum. Richmond — Charlotte Alling, David Hahn, Museum of the Confederacy.

Washington, D.C.: Preston E. Amos; Deborah Edge, National Archives and Record Service; Evelyn Nave, Photoduplication Service, Library of Congress.

The index was prepared by Roy Nanovic.

BIBLIOGRAPHY

Books

Abbot, Henry L., *Siege Artillery in the Campaigns against Richmond, with Notes on the 15-Inch Gun.* Washington, D.C.: GPO, 1867.

Albert, Allen, ed., *History of the Forty-Fifth Regiment Pennsylvania Veteran Volunteer Infantry 1861-1865.* Williamsport, Pa.: Grit Publishing Co., 1912.

Alexander, E. P., *Military Memoirs of a Confederate.* Dayton: Morningside Bookshop, 1977 (reprint of 1907 edition).

Anderson, John, *The Fifty-Seventh Regiment of Massachusetts Volunteers in the War of the Rebellion, Army of the Potomac.* Boston: E. B. Stillings & Co., 1896.

Beale, R.L.T., *History of the Ninth Virginia Cavalry.* Richmond: B. F. Johnson Publishing Co., 1899.

Bernard, George S., comp. and ed., *War Talks of Confederate Veterans.* Dayton: Morningside Bookshop, 1981 (reprint of 1892 edition).

Bosbyshell, Oliver Christian, *The 48th in the War.* Philadelphia: Avil Printing Co., 1895.

Caldwell, J.F.J., *The History of a Brigade of South Carolinians, Known First as "Gregg's" and Subsequently as "McGowan's Brigade."* Philadelphia: King & Baird, 1866.

Calos, Mary Mitchell, Charlotte Easterling and Ella Sue Rayburn, *Old City Point and Hopewell: The First 370 Years.* Norfolk, Va.: The Donning Co., 1983.

Carter, Robert Goldthwaite, *Four Brothers in Blue.* Austin: University of Texas Press, 1978.

Catton, Bruce:

Grant Takes Command. Boston: Little, Brown, 1968.

A Stillness at Appomattox. Garden City, N.Y.: Doubleday, 1954.

Coggins, Jack, *Arms and Equipment of the Civil War.* Garden City, N.Y.: Doubleday, 1962.

Cresap, Bernarr, *Appomattox Commander: The Story of General E.O.C. Ord.* San Diego: A. S. Barnes & Co., 1981.

Cushman, Frederick E., *History of the 58th Regt. Massachusetts Vols.* Washington, D.C.: Gibson Brothers, 1865.

Dickert, D. Augustus, *History of Kershaw's Brigade.* Dayton: Morningside Bookshop, 1976 (reprint of 1899 edition).

Dunlop, W. S., *Lee's Sharpshooters: The Forefront of Battle.* Dayton: Morningside Bookshop, 1982.

Frassanito, William A., *Grant and Lee: The Virginia Campaigns, 1864-1865.* New York: Charles Scribner's Sons, 1983.

Freeman, Douglas Southall:

Gettysburg to Appomattox. Vol. 3 of *Lee's Lieutenants: A Study in Command.* New York: Charles Scribner's Sons, 1944.

R. E. Lee: A Biography. Vol. 3. New York: Charles Scribner's Sons, 1935.

Gibbon, John, *Personal Recollections of the Civil War.* Dayton: Morningside Bookshop, 1978 (reprint of 1928 edition).

Gibbs, James M., comp., *History of the First Battalion Pennsylvania Six Months Volunteers and 187th Regiment Pennsylvania Volunteer Infantry.* Harrisburg, Pa.: Central Printing and Publishing, 1905.

Goldsborough, W. W., *The Maryland Line in the Confederate Army: 1861-1865.* Gaithersburg, Md.: Butternut Press, 1983 (reprint of 1900 edition).

Gould, Joseph, *The Story of the Forty-Eighth.* Philadelphia: Forty-Eighth Regiment Pennsylvania Veteran Volunteer Infantry Association, 1908.

Grant, U. S., *Personal Memoirs of U. S. Grant.* Ed. by E. B. Long. New York: Da Capo Press, 1952.

Haskell, John Cheves, *The Haskell Memoirs.* Ed. by Gilbert E. Govan and James W. Livingood. New York: G. P. Putnam's Sons, 1960.

Heth, Henry, *The Memoirs of Henry Heth.* Ed. by James L. Morrison Jr. Westport, Conn.: Greenwood Press, 1974.

Holzman, Robert S., *Stormy Ben Butler.* New York: The Macmillan Co., 1954.

Humphreys, Andrew A., *The Virginia Campaign of '64 and '65.* Vol. 12 of *Campaigns of the Civil War.* New York: Charles Scribner's Sons, 1883.

Johnson, Robert Underwood, and Clarence Clough Buel, eds., *Battles and Leaders of the Civil War.* Vol. 4. New York: Thomas Yoseloff, 1956.

Kirk, Hyland C., *Heavy Guns and Light: A History of the 4th New York Heavy Artillery.* New York: C. T. Dillingham, 1890.

Lebsock, Suzanne, *The Free Women of Petersburg: Status and Culture in a Southern Town, 1784-1860.* New York: Norton, 1984.

Lee, R. E., *The Wartime Papers of R. E. Lee.* Ed. by Clifford Dowdey. New York: Bramhall House, 1961.

Livermore, Thomas L., *Days and Events 1860-1866.* Boston: Houghton Mifflin, 1920.

Lyman, Theodore, *Meade's Headquarters 1863-1865: Letters of Colonel Theodore Lyman from the Wilderness to Appomattox.* Ed. by George R. Agassiz. Boston: The Atlantic Monthly Press, 1922.

McAllister, Robert, *The Civil War Letters of General Robert McAllister.* Ed. by James I. Robertson Jr. New Brunswick, N.J.: Rutgers University Press, 1965.

McCausland, Elizabeth, *The Life and Work of Edward Lamson Henry N.A. 1841-1919.* New York: Kennedy Graphics, Inc. and Da Capo Press, 1970.

Meade, George, *The Life and Letters of George Gordon Meade.* Vol. 2. Ed. by George Gordon Meade. New York: Charles Scribner's Sons, 1913.

Military Order of the Loyal Legion of the United States, Commandery of the State of Illinois, *Military Essays and Recollections.* Vol. 3. Chicago: The Dial Press, 1899.

Military Order of the Loyal Legion of the United States, The Michigan Commandery, *War Papers.* Vol. 2. Detroit: The Michigan Commandery, 1898.

Muffly, J. W., ed., *The Story of Our Regiment: A History of the 148th Pennsylvania Vols.* Des Moines: Kenyon Printing, 1904.

Oates, William C., *The War between the Union and the Confederacy.* Dayton: Morningside Bookshop, 1974 (reprint of 1905 edition).

Owen, Wm. Miller, *In Camp and Battle with the Washington Artillery of New Orleans.* Boston: Ticknor and Co., 1885.

Porter, Horace, *Campaigning with Grant.* New York: The Century Co., 1897.

Preston, N. D., *History of the Tenth Regiment of Cavalry New York State Volunteers.* New York: D. Appleton and Co., 1892.

Pullen, John J., *The Twentieth Maine: A Volunteer Regiment in the Civil War.* Dayton: Morningside Bookshop, 1980.

Pyne, Henry R., *Ride to War: The History of the First New Jersey Cavalry.* Ed. by Earl Schenck Miers. New Brunswick, N.J.: Rutgers University Press, 1961.

Ripley, Edward Hastings, *Vermont General: The Unusual War Experiences of Edward Hastings Ripley.* Ed. by Otto Eisenschiml. New York: The Devin-Adair Co., 1960.

Roe, Alfred S., *The Thirty-Ninth Regiment Massachusetts Volunteers 1862-1865.* Worcester, Mass.: Regimental Veteran Association, 1914.

Shaw, Horace H., and Charles J. House, *The First Maine Heavy Artillery 1862-1865.* Portland, Me.: Privately published, 1903.

Sheridan, P. H., *Personal Memoirs of P. H. Sheridan.* Vol. 1. St. Clair Shores, Mich.: Scholarly Press, 1977 (reprint of 1888 edition).

Simpson, Harold B., *Hood's Texas Brigade: Lee's Grenadier Guard.* Dallas: Alcor Publishing Co., 1983.

Sommers, Richard J., *Richmond Redeemed: The Siege at Petersburg.* Garden City, N.Y.: Doubleday, 1981.

Starr, Stephen Z., *The War in the East from Gettysburg to Appomattox 1863-1865.* Vol. 2 of *The Union Cavalry in the Civil War.* Baton Rouge: Louisiana State University Press, 1981.

Stiles, Robert, *Four Years under Marse Robert.* Dayton: Morningside Bookshop, 1977 (reprint of 1903 edition).

Tucker, Glenn, *Hancock the Superb.* Dayton: Morningside Bookshop, 1980.

United States War Department, *War of the Rebellion: A Compilation of the Official Records of the Union and Confederate Armies.* Series 1:

Vol. 36, Parts 1-3. Washington, D.C.: GPO, 1891.

Vol. 40, Parts 1-3. Washington, D.C.: GPO, 1892.

Vol. 42, Part 2. Washington, D.C.: GPO, 1893.

Wainwright, Charles S., *A Diary of Battle.* Ed. by Allan Nevins. New York: Harcourt, Brace & World, 1962.

Walker, Francis A., *History of the Second Army Corps in the Army of the Potomac.* New York: Charles Scribner's Sons, 1886.

Wallace, Willard M., *Soul of the Lion: General Joshua L. Chamberlain.* New York: Thomas Nelson & Sons, 1960.

Ward, George W., *History of the Second Pennsylvania Veteran Heavy Artillery (112th Regiment Pennsylvania Volunteers), from 1861 to 1866.* Philadelphia: George W. Ward, 1904.

Wise, Jennings Cropper, *The Long Arm of Lee: The History of the Artillery of the Army of Northern Virginia.* New York: Oxford University Press, 1959.

Wise, John Sergeant, *The End of an Era.* Boston: Houghton, Mifflin and Co., 1900.

Other Sources

Bates, Delevan, and Fred S. Bowley, "A Day with the Colored Troops." *The National Tribune*, January 30, 1908.

"Before Petersburg." *Harper's Weekly*, August 20, 1864.

Butowsky, Harry, "Appomattox Manor-City Point." Unpublished thesis. National Park Service, 1978.

Coates, Earl J., "The Bloody First Maine." *Civil War Times Illustrated*, July 1972.

Cross, Thomas H., "Battle of the Crater." *The National Tribune*, February 25, 1882.

Cullen, Joseph P., "The Siege of Petersburg." Philadelphia: Eastern Acorn Press, 1981.

Dawley, Free S., "The Crater." *The National Tribune*, November 6, 1884.

"General Warren's Raid," *Harper's Weekly*, December 31, 1864.

Gladstone, William, "Civil War Photo Maps." *Military Images Magazine*, September-October, 1982.

Longacre, Edward G.:
"The Petersburg Follies." *Civil War Times Illustrated*, January 1980.
"Wilson-Kautz Raid." *Civil War Times Illustrated*, May 1970.

McMaster, Frederick W., "The Battle of the Crater." *Southern Historical Society Papers*, Vol. 10.

Peabody, Frank E., "Crossing of the James and First Assault upon Petersburg, June 12-15, 1864." *Papers of the Military Historical Society of Massachusetts*, 1900.

Preston, N. D., "Trevellian Station." *The National Tribune*, January 5, 1888.

Proctor, D. E., and D. H. Wilton, "The Massacre at the Crater." *The National Tribune*, October 17, 1907.

Ropes, John C., "The Failure to Take Petersburg on June 16-18, 1864." *Papers of the Military Historical Society of Massachusetts*, 1879.

Roulhac, Thomas R., "The Forty-Ninth North Carolina Infantry, C.S.A." *Southern Historical Society Papers*, Vol. 23.

Stedman, Charles M., "Battle at Reams's Station." *Southern Historical Society Papers*, Vol. 19.

Stewart, Wm. H., "The Charge of the Crater." *Southern Historical Society Papers*, Vol. 25.

White, Daniel, "Charging the Crater." *The National Tribune*, June 21, 1883.

PICTURE CREDITS

The sources for the illustrations in this book are shown below. Credits from left to right are separated by semicolons, from top to bottom by dashes.

Cover: Library of Congress. 2, 3: Maps by Peter McGinn. 8: Painting by William Maury Robertson, Centre Hill Mansion, Petersburg, Va., photographed by Larry Sherer. 9: Paintings by William Skinner Simpson, father or son, Fort Henry Branch of the Association for the Preservation of Virginia Antiquities (APVA), courtesy Siege Museum, Petersburg, Va., photographed by Larry Sherer. 10, 11: Paintings by William Skinner Simpson, father or son, Fort Henry Branch of APVA, courtesy Siege Museum, Petersburg, Va. (2); painting by William Skinner Simpson, father or son, courtesy Francis M. Gilliam — painting by William Skinner Simpson, father or son, courtesy Francis M. Gilliam, all photographed by Larry Sherer. 12, 13: Paintings by William Skinner Simpson, father or son, Fort Henry Branch of APVA, courtesy Siege Museum, Petersburg, Va., except bottom right, painting by William Skinner Simpson, father or son, courtesy Francis M. Gilliam, all photographed by Larry Sherer. 14, 15: Painting by William Skinner Simpson, father or son, Fort Henry Branch of APVA, courtesy Siege Museum, Petersburg, Va., photographed by Ronald H. Jennings — painting by William Maury Robertson, courtesy Centre Hill Mansion, Petersburg, Va., photographed by Larry Sherer; paintings by William Skinner Simpson, father or son, Fort Henry Branch of APVA, courtesy Siege Museum, Petersburg, Va., photographed by Larry Sherer (2). 17: Library of Congress. 18, 19: Virginia State Library. 20, 21: Library of Congress. 23: Massachusetts Commandery of the Military Order of the Loyal Legion of the United States and the U.S. Army Military History Institute (MASS-MOLLUS/USAMHI), copied by A. Pierce Bounds. 24, 25: Painting by James E. Taylor, Library of Congress. 26: The Museum of the Confederacy, Richmond. 28, 29: Courtesy Brian Pohanka; from *Reminiscences of the War of the Rebellion, 1861-1865*, by Elbridge J. Copp, published by the author, 1911; courtesy Bill Turner (2); MASS-MOLLUS/USAMHI, copied by A. Pierce Bounds; courtesy Harris J. Andrews, copied by Larry Sherer — Library of Congress. 30, 31: Drawing by Alfred R. Waud, Library of Congress; Library of Congress. 32: The Western Reserve Historical Society, Cleveland; National Archives Neg. No. 111-B-4300; MASS-MOLLUS/USAMHI, copied by A. Pierce Bounds. 33: Courtesy Bill Turner; Valentine Museum, Richmond. 35: The J. Howard Wert Gettysburg Collection and Civil War Antiquities, photographed by Larry Sherer. 37: Library of Congress. 38: MASS-MOLLUS/USAMHI, copied by A. Pierce Bounds. 40: Map by William L. Hezlep. 41: National Archives Neg. No. 111-B-5176. 42, 43: National Park Service (NPS), Petersburg National Battlefield Museum — drawings by Edwin Forbes, Library of Congress (3). 45: Courtesy Bill Turner. 46, 47: Courtesy Bill Turner — National Archives Neg. No. 111-B-347. 49: Drawing by Frank Vizetelly by permission of the Houghton Library. 51: National Archives Neg. No. 111-B-4372 — Bowdoin College Library, Brunswick, Me., photographed by Dennis Griggs. 52: National Archives Neg. No. 111-B-163. 54, 55: Drawing by Alfred R. Waud, Library of Congress; courtesy Larry B. Williford. 57: Courtesy Frank & Marie-T. Wood Print Collections, Alexandria, Va. 58, 59: Maine State Museum, photographed by Gregory Hart; from *Armies and Leaders*, Vol. 10 of *The Photographic History of the Civil War*, edited by Francis Trevelyan Miller, published by The Review of Reviews Co., New York, 1912 — from *The First Maine Heavy Artillery 1862-1865*, by Horace H. Shaw and Charles J. House, privately published, Portland, Me., 1903. 60, 61: Courtesy Robert G. Borrell Sr., photographed by Michael Latil (2); from *The First Maine Heavy Artillery 1862-1865*, by Horace H. Shaw and Charles J. House, privately published, Portland, Me., 1903 — drawing by Edwin Forbes, Library of Congress. 62, 63: From *The First Maine Heavy Artillery 1862-1865*, by Horace H. Shaw and Charles J. House, privately published, Portland, Me., 1903. 65: NPS, Petersburg National Battlefield Museum, photographed by Larry Sherer. 66: Dementi Studios, Richmond. 69: From *Battles and Leaders of the Civil War*, Vol. 4, published by The Century Co., New York, 1887. 70: From *The Tragedy of the Crater*, by Henry Pleasants Jr., published by The Christopher Publishing House, Boston, 1938. 71: Courtesy Frank & Marie-T. Wood Print Collections, Alexandria, Va. 72: Map by Walter W. Roberts. 73: Library of Congress. 74: MASS-MOLLUS/USAMHI, copied by A. Pierce Bounds. 76, 77: Drawing by Alfred R. Waud, Private Collection. 78: National Archives Neg. No. 111-B-4591. 79: Map by Walter W. Roberts. 80: National Archives Neg. No. 111-B-4296; Library of Congress. 81: Courtesy Frank & Marie-T. Wood Print Collections, Alexandria, Va. 82: MASS-MOLLUS/USAMHI, copied by A. Pierce Bounds. 83: MASS-MOLLUS/USAMHI, copied by A. Pierce Bounds — courtesy Bill Turner. 84, 85: Flagstaff, Siege Museum, Petersburg, Va., photographed by Larry Sherer; flag, Museum of the Confederacy, Richmond, photographed by Ronald H. Jennings; painting by H. E. Gassman after James A. Elder, Siege Museum, Petersburg, Va., photographed by Ronald H. Jennings. 86: From *The Haskell Memoirs*, by John Cheves Haskell, edited by Gilbert E. Govan and James W. Livingood, published by G. P. Putnam's Sons, New York, 1960. 87: NPS, Petersburg National Battlefield Museum, photographed by Larry Sherer. 88, 89: Courtesy Frank & Marie-T. Wood Print Collections, Alexandria, Va.; MASS-MOLLUS/USAMHI, copied by A. Pierce Bounds. 90-93: Background engravings from *The American Soldier in the Civil War*, by Frank Leslie, published by Bryan, Taylor & Co., New York, 1895, all artifacts from NPS, Petersburg National Battlefield Museum, photographed by Larry Sherer, except box, page 90, photographed by Mike Wiltshire. 95: Courtesy Chris Calkins, photographed by Larry Sherer. 96: Map by William L. Hezlep. 98: From *The War between the Union and the Confederacy*, by William C. Oates, published by The Neale Publishing Co., New York, 1905. 99: Courtesy Bill Turner. 100: Library of Congress. 101: Museum of Pennsylvania (PHMC), copied by A. Pierce Bounds. 102: Museum of the Confederacy, Richmond; courtesy William Gladstone Collection; Library of Congress. 104: MASS-MOLLUS/USAMHI, copied by A. Pierce Bounds. 105: National Archives Neg. No. 111-B-37. 106, 107: Courtesy Kenneth M. Newman, The Old Print Shop, New York, photographed by Henry Groskinsky. 109: Painting by James R. Lambdin, courtesy Chicago Historical Society. 110: National Archives Neg. No. 111-B-4187. 111: Library of Congress. 112, 113: Siege Museum, Petersburg, Va., photographed by Larry Sherer, inset National Archives Neg. No. 111-B-425. 114, 115: Sketch by Alfred R. Waud, Library of Congress, inset Museum of the Confederacy, Richmond. 116, 117: The Edward L. Bafford Photography Collection, Albin O. Kuhn Library and Gallery, University of Maryland Baltimore County, copied by Alan M. Scherr; painting by André Castaigne, West Point Museum Collection, U.S. Military Academy, photographed by Henry Groskinsky. 118, 119: Courtesy Frank & Marie-T. Wood Print Collections, Alexandria, Va.; courtesy William Gladstone Collection, copied by Michael Latil. 120, 121: Courtesy William Gladstone Collection; courtesy Milwaukee Public Museum; Library of Congress — Valentine Museum, Richmond. 122, 123: Library of Congress — courtesy Frank & Marie-T. Wood Print Collections, Alexandria, Va.; L. M. Strayer Collection, copied by Brian Blauser. 124: Library of Congress, courtesy Preston E. Amos, except medal, courtesy The Institute of Heraldry, U.S. Army, photographed by Ned McCormick. 125: Library of Congress; Library of Congress, courtesy Preston E. Amos (3). 126, 127: Drawing by Fred Holz — Library of Congress. 128-133: Library of Congress. 134, 135: Library of

Congress (2) — National Archives Neg. No. 111-B-768. 137: Siege Museum, Petersburg, Va., photographed by Larry Sherer. 138: Library of Congress. 140, 141: Drawing by Alfred R. Waud, Siege Museum, Petersburg, Va., photographed by Larry Sherer. 142, 143: Library of Congress. 144: State Historical Society of Wisconsin. 147: Painting by Benjamin Clinedinst West from *Campaigning with Grant*, by Horace Porter, published by The Century Co., New York, 1897. 148: Courtesy Frank & Marie-T. Wood Print Collections, Alexandria, Va. 151: Painting by William Ludwell Shepard, Museum of the Confederacy, Richmond, photographed by Larry Sherer. 152, 153: Courtesy Frank & Marie-T. Wood Print Collections, Alexandria, Va. 155: Drawing by William Waud, Library of Congress. 157: Museum of the Confederacy, Richmond, photographed by Ronald H. Jennings — from *The Venturers, The Hampton, Harrison and Earle Families of Virginia*, *South Carolina and Texas*, by Virginia G. Meynard, published by Southern Historical Press, Inc., 1981. 159: Painting by Winslow Homer, The Detroit Institute of Arts, Gift of Dexter M. Ferry Jr. 160, 161: National Archives Neg. No. 111-B-152 — painting by Edward Lamson Henry, Addison Gallery of American Art, Phillips Academy, Andover, Mass., photographed by Henry Groskinsky. 162, 163: Detail of painting by Edward Lamson Henry, Addison Gallery of American Art, Phillips Academy, Andover, Mass., photographed by Henry Groskinsky; Boston Athenaeum — Library of Congress (2). 164, 165: Albert Shaw Collection, Review of Reviews *Photographic History of the Civil War*, copied by Larry Sherer; detail of painting by Edward Lamson Henry, Addison Gallery of American Art, Phillips Academy, Andover, Mass., photographed by Henry Groskinsky — Library of Congress; The Western Reserve Historical Society, Cleveland. 166, 167: Detail of painting by Edward Lamson Henry, Addison Gallery of American Art, Phillips Academy, Andover, Mass., photographed by Henry Groskinsky; Library of Congress — The Western Reserve Historical Society, Cleveland; courtesy Joe Buberger/USAMHI, copied by A. Pierce Bounds. 168, 169: Library of Congress; detail of painting by Edward Lamson Henry, Addison Gallery of American Art, Phillips Academy, Andover, Mass., photographed by Henry Groskinsky — NPS, Petersburg National Battlefield Museum; Library of Congress. 170, 171: Detail of painting by Edward Lamson Henry, Addison Gallery of American Art, Phillips Academy, Andover, Mass., photographed by Henry Groskinsky — from *Forts and Artillery*, Vol. 5 of *The Photographic History of the Civil War*, edited by Francis Trevelyan Miller, published by The Review of Reviews Co., 1912; Library of Congress — National Archives Neg. No. 111-B-4769.

INDEX

Numerals in italics indicate an illustration of the subject mentioned.